To My Three Girls
Amanda, Charlotte and Mom

ACKNOWLEDGMENT

I would like to thank my family and friends for giving me good material to write about. I try to look at every situation in life with humor. I was lucky to have wonderful parents, Jack and Helen Wayman. I would like to thank them for their unconditional love and support. They taught me traditional, old fashion, small town values that make me who I am. Also, I would like to thank my only brother, Garry Wayman, and his family who have always been there for me when I needed them.

I would like to thank my Lord and Savior Jesus Christ for calling me into His wonderful family. I would like to thank the families at Grace Bible Chapel for accepting me as a son when I first came to Springfield in my twenties. I had no family here and only knew a few people. The families at Grace Bible Chapel became my Springfield family. I would like to specifically thank the families of Bob Isringhausen and Phil Dossett. They really helped me a great deal in life.

I would like to thank all my political friends over the years that have given me a lot of material for this book, from President Nixon to my county chairman Ron Summers. I would like to thank my good friend, Gary Strohm, for talking me into coming to Springfield and helping me get my first job with the Secretary of State.

To my friends at the Secretary of State, thanks for putting up with me for over 20 years. To my bosses, thanks for helping me become a better manager. To my coworkers, thanks for your patience with me and for making me look good. To our current Secretary of State Jesse White, the only Democrat I have ever worked for, thanks for being such a super guy and treating everyone, including left over Republicans, fairly and with respect.

TABLE OF CONTENTS

INTRODUCTION

I'm the kind of guy who can't do my business without reading something. I was so tired of reading magazines or newspapers; I thought there had to be another way. How come there are not specific bathroom books? Books that do not continue, books that can be read one story at a time in about the amount of time it takes an average person to do their business? We all have to spend a certain amount of time each day on the can, right?

With that, I thought of writing this book.

While You Do Your Business is intended to be read in the bathroom while you are doing your business. Each story stands alone and can be read in the average amount of time that it takes the average person to go.

However, you may read this book away from the toilet, while sitting on a sofa or in your favorite chair, or while riding in an airplane, or while relaxing in the park. There will be no book cops around to arrest you, so feel free to read it anywhere, at anytime, day or night.

For the record, I have always been a storyteller. This book is an accumulation of my best stories. Everything in the book is true or at least based on facts. I have changed names in some of the stories, to protect the innocent, and to prevent law suits.

I hope you will find my stories funny, motivational, interesting and everything else. I hope you tell your friends, and your neighbors.

CHAPTER 1

START YOUR DAY WITH A LAUGH

We should start each day with a shower, bacon and eggs, orange juice and a laugh! The big breakfast will make you go to that special room, the smallest room in the house, to spend a few minutes to do your business. While there, you can read these stories that will start your day off with a laugh.

BUFFY – "HOW ABOUT A BOILED EGG?"

This story is about a gal, let's call her "Buffy," who met every preconceived bias you may have of a "Buffy." Buffy was the only daughter of a wealthy businessman. He wanted his daughter to get some experience in the workplace. Buffy was a very attractive blond who wanted to be a model. This was the first job she had. In fact, we later learned that she had not experienced much in life.

On Buffy's first day on the job, she brought in her modeling portfolio, which included several photos that at least should have had an "R" rating. She proudly displayed her photos and asked several of us if we wanted one to display on our desks. As a joke, I actually took one and put it on my desk. A few days later, I was kidding her and implied that the boss was kind of hurt because she hadn't asked him if he wanted a photo. The next day she came to work all excited. She brought the boss a gift all wrapped up with a nice ribbon. You know what it was? It was a picture of her in a nice frame. She proudly marched into the boss' office and gave it to him. Let's say we had a big private laugh and the boss' wife and kids didn't appreciate it.

Her job was to work in the secretarial pool in the administrative area right outside the boss' office. One day, I was in the boss' office talking about a project when we heard the telephone ringing. We looked out of the office and Buffy was just sitting at her desk by herself doing her nails. After about ten rings, my boss got out of his desk and walked to the secretarial pool area. "Aren't you going to answer the phone?" he said. Her response was, "Oh, am I suppose to?" Since the other girls were usually there with her, no one had specifically told her to answer the phone while they were gone. She had no common sense.

She really took advantage of each idle moment. Her boyfriend's name was Todd. She would write on paper, "I love Todd, Todd loves me, I love Todd, Todd loves me," over and over. One day we found about 50 full pages of this in the waste basket! What talent!?

One day she had indicated that she was hungry and wanted to try something new during break. She asked what type of food they had in our cafeteria. We told her a few of the items on the menu, including hard-boiled eggs. Buffy and her father had a maid, who did all of the cooking, so Buffy had not had much experience in the kitchen. She said that she had not had a hard-boiled egg before, and that their maid always cooked her eggs scrambled. So with that, Buffy decided to go out on the limb and try something new.

After her break was over, we asked her if she liked the hard-boiled egg. Her reply was "No, not really. I thought it was too crunchy!" We looked at each other with amazement. "Crunchy! Did you not peel the egg?" we asked. Her response was "Was I suppose to peel it!"

THE CHICAGO PUBLIC LIBRARY RULES – "CRIMINALS BEWARE!"

During a recent visit to the Chicago Public Library, I was taken in by a list of rules posted on the wall there. Knowing that these rules would really take "a bite out of crime," I wanted to do my part for society and share them with you. I present these rules to you as they really appeared, quoted directly with no exaggeration. This is the honest to God truth!

· · · · · · ·

The Chicago Public Library
Guidelines Governing the Use of the Library

PLEASE DO NOT:

1. Engage in any illegal activity or behavior
2. Vandalize library facilities, equipment or materials
3. Bring in animals except guide dogs
4. Harass other library users or library staff (physical, sexual or verbal abuse)
5. Eat, drink, smoke or sleep
6. Bathe, shave or wash clothes
7. Remove library materials from the building without charging them out

PERSONS WHO FAIL TO OBSERVE THESE
GUIDELINES MAY BE ASKED TO LEAVE
THE BUILDING OR BE SUBJECT TO AR-
REST.

• • • • • • • •

Can you believe these rules? What a way to stop
crime? I am sure any potential violator will think
twice before attempting to commit one of those in-
fractions. They have the strong arm of the Chicago
Library Authority to stop them.

Each rule deserves individual comment, so let's start
from the beginning. First, I am glad the Chicago
Public Library used the words "Please do not." The
politeness of the library is appreciated. People do not
always say "Please" when they should. I am sure that
politeness will go a long way in the "Windy City."
Potential violators may stop their behavior in their
tracks if they are politely asked not to. I think that
our U.S. Criminal Justice system could learn a lesson
from the Chicago Public Library!

The first rule covers everything wrong and illegal. It
reads: "Please do not engage in any illegal activity or
behavior." This covers it all. I am sure that criminals
would appreciate this commandment. It would also
prevent anyone from going before a judge and saying, "Your honor, I just didn't know it was wrong to
shoot the librarian." Instead, the criminals are told up
front with the rules clearly posted on the wall. Any-

thing that is illegal is prohibited in the library. They must conduct their illegal activity outside.

In case one would not understand or recognize that vandalism is an illegal activity, the library clearly mentions this in the second rule. It states: "Please do not vandalize library facilities, equipment or materials." In other words, do not destroy any of their property. This would include the library itself, any computers or other equipment or any of the books.

I am sure that it is necessary to let people know about the anti-vandalism bias of the library. These days, some people just take these things for granted. In fact, I was thinking about busting one of the computers myself during my visit, until I saw the rule. I immediately corrected myself and remembered that they said "Please."

The third rule actually made sense to me. It states, "Please do not bring in animals except guide dogs." I know that some people just think they can bring their dogs anywhere. I am sure that the libraries would be full of barking dogs and meowing cats if it wasn't for this rule. I was also wondering how a blind person could read this rule. Perhaps they should post it in Braille.

The next rule asks us not to "harass other library users or library staff (physical, sexual or verbal abuse.)" In case one does not know what type of harassment they are talking about, the library specifically identifies it for you. You can't get physical, you can't get sexual and you can't get verbal in the library. If you do, you are harassing the staff or other library users.

I'm glad they identified who you can not harass. I guess if you are not on the staff or a library user, you are fair game. I just stopped by to use the bathroom and get a drink of water, so I'm not sure how I would be identified. Am I a library user? I'm not using the book part of the library, but I am using the facilities. I would have to ask on that one.

However, sexual harassment is clearly identified. If one begins to sexually harass the librarian, then she can point to rule number four. "Didn't you read the rules; you can't put your hand up my dress!"

"Please do not eat, drink, smoke or sleep." This rule is not fair! I think there is nothing wrong with sleeping in a library, unless you are snoring. Taking a nap between books does not hurt anyone. I think the constitution should give us the right to sleep in libraries. In fact, just reading the constitution would put most people to sleep. If one brings in a pillow, blanket, changes to their pajamas and sleeps for eight hours, I would understand why that would be wrong. However, sleeping in general should not be prohibited. (I think I will write the library and complain!)

How about eating and drinking? That does not make sense at all to me. How would one define eating? Are they talking about candy or a full course meal? I would understand not bringing in a pizza or something, but "eating" is really a broad term. Drinking? If you can't drink, then why is there a water fountain in the library? Would you explain that to me? I think the library needs to clarify this rule like they did with the seeing eye dog.

This brings us to the next rule: "Please do not bathe, shave or wash clothes." Remember this because if you want to take a bath in the library's sink, you can't! (After all, I didn't see any showers in the restroom.) I don't know about you, but it has always been one of my fantasies to take a bath in a library. And, if you want to do your laundry there, think again; you will have to visit your local laundromat.

The last rule, "Please do not remove library materials from the building without charging them out," I think this should go without saying. Isn't this what a library is all about anyway? But, in case one has not ever heard of the library system of checking out books, it is there in the list of rules.

The guidelines end with the statement that if people do not obey the rules they "may be asked to leave the building or be subject to arrest." It is either or. Either you leave or you are arrested. I guess that if you engage in any criminal activity and then leave, then you are ok. You will only be arrested if you refuse to leave. So, criminals or rule breakers, keep this in mind. If you shoot the librarian or vandalize their property, and then leave, you will not be subject to arrest. You will only be arrested if you stay in the library.

Criminals in Chicago, beware of the public library. They will not take any crap from anyone! They have their own Library Rules!

SMALL TOWN PRIDE - "DARN PROUD TO BE FROM BENTON!"

People are motivated for different reasons. Some say that the American Spirit lives within us and lifts us to new highs. We all should be proud of our heritage, regardless of where we are from. For example, some may be proud to be Native American or African American. Most of us are proud to be Americans. Others may just be proud of their families. For me, I am proud of the small town that I was born and raised in.

The small Southern Illinois town that I am talking about is Benton. I left Benton for college when I was 18 years old and never lived there again. However, my roots are there and the way I see life is through that small town.

Benton is a small town in Franklin County, Illinois. The population is only 7,000 give or take a few. The people from Benton are quite proud of their history. We are also quite proud of the celebrities who call Benton their home. In fact, for a town so small, you will be amazed how many famous people have been raised there.

John Malkovich, the actor from the movies "In the Line of Fire," "Dangerous Liaisons," and "Places in the Heart," was born there. His family still lives there. In fact, his brother is the editor of the local newspaper. You may have heard John talk about his brother, Danny, on various TV talk shows. Once on

Saturday Night Live, John's entire monologue was about growing up in Benton.

In fact, John has not forgotten his roots. He is often seen walking down the streets of Benton, visiting relatives and friends. I think he may often think of that small town as he uses his creative talents in motion pictures.

When thinking of motivation, one can't forget sports. The spirit of pride for your team or country will often motivate players as they go for the gold. Former U.S. Olympic Basketball Team member Doug Collins is from Benton. Doug is the former coach of the Chicago Bulls and Detroit Pistons, a former NBA player himself, and current sports TV broadcaster.

Doug's father was a former sheriff for the county. In fact, his mother currently lives three houses down from my mother. Now I know I got your attention. You must be really impressed? Just think, a book written by the neighbor of the mother of a celebrity! (I should put that in my biography.)

Other famous people from Benton are listed on my web site http://www.gordonwayman.com. They include the rock group Revis, funny guy professional comedian Tommy Johnagin, Grand Ole Opry Member Billy Grammar, and former NBC Vice President Lynn Bolin.

My mother, Helen Wayman, gave me a booklet titled, "The Heritage of Franklin County Illinois," written in 1964 by Susie M. Ramsey and Flossie P. Miller. (I say booklet because it looks likc it was typed on a typewriter, Xeroxed off, and placed in a book format.

What do you expect from such a small town?) The book is currently distributed by the Franklin County Historical Society. The book is full of Franklin County history. It is a book full of information on famous people from Benton (prior to 1964–they could not see into the future), along with various historical facts. Some of the information included in the book is quite interesting, such as:

The last legal hanging in Illinois took place in Benton when gangster Charlie Birger was hanged. Birger was arrested and held in the Franklin County Jail for one year before his hanging. You can tour the jail cell today. He was actually hanged on the public square, and the platform is proudly on display, and;

John A. Logan, a Civil War General from Benton, and candidate for vice president of the United States, came up with the idea for Memorial Day. The story has it that he was giving a speech at a graveyard and a flower from a tree fell upon a grave. This gave him the idea to decorate graves and have a holiday to honor those who died in wars. (So, when you have an extra day off work with pay in May, you can thank Benton's native son.)

All that seemed to be on the up and up, very legitimate historical facts that the county can be proud of. However, I think they went too far on a couple of historical items listed in the book. For example:

"Mrs. Julie Hickman, Dr. Z. Hickman's wife was the first woman in Benton to subscribe to the Ladies Home Journal." They went on to say, "Dr. Hickman thought his wife was too extravagant." Well, I can imagine. A subscription to a magazine exclusively for women, what was Julie thinking?

The "First toilet soap was used in the A.D. Jacon home." I wonder how they found this out? I guess there must have been quite an odor in the rest of the town's bathrooms.

"The first woman to wear a silk waist in Benton was Florence Hudson." Hum, that sounds interesting. Boy, I bet Florence's parents must have been so proud!

"Susie M. Ramsey was the first lady president of a Benton vicinity cemetery, the New Union Cemetery, in 1956." Susie was one of the writers of this historical book. Now, maybe that explains it. A lady president of a cemetery? What does a cemetery president do? And, a Union one? The "New" Union Cemetery, didn't the civil war occur in the 1800s? How can a cemetery be "new"? Did they move the graves or what?

"The first woman to have a hair permanent was Mrs. Jess Diamond." And that's not all, "The first Benton schoolteacher with a permanent was Mary Hart." Wow this book doesn't miss a thing!

They go on and on. They have the names of the first person to do about anything you can imagine. The first radio, the first TV, the first stove, the first bathroom, it's all there. Everything you could imagine. It must have taken the writers years to come up with all of these useful facts. And the price of that wonderful book was only $5, what a bargain!

Politics has always been a popular thing in Franklin County. Anyone who's anyone is active in the Democratic Party. The writers of this great book were no exception. You can tell the writers really loved President John F. Kennedy. You can tell that Kennedy's assassination was on their minds when they wrote the book, because every chance they got, they added something about JFK. For example, and I quote:

"On May 29, 1964, a five-cent stamp was issued honoring the thirty-fifth President of the United States, John F. Kennedy, on what would have been his forty-seventh birthday. There were sixteen designs submitted to Mrs. Jacqueline Kennedy, who had the final selection. Collectors show more interest now than when the tradition started, with the issuing of the Lincoln stamp after his assassination." First of all, when they wrote about the 16 designs, I thought they would say that one of the 16 was submitted by a Franklin County resident or something, but no–nothing. They just had to put in that fact. Second, how did they know that more interest was shown with the Kennedy stamp than the Lincoln stamp? I guess it was just another way to say the "Democrats Rule!"

My favorite quote is also about Kennedy. And no, I am not making this up. It reads: "President Kennedy's assassination on November 22, 1963, was a sad day for the county. President Kennedy had not visited in Franklin County, but no doubt he flew over the county en route to the adjoining county, when he visited in Herrin, Illinois." Wow! Isn't that something to be proud of! So, if you ever visit Franklin County, you can feel proud that President Kennedy, "no doubt" flew over the county. I think we should cash in on that historical fact! I can see a sign now, "Welcome to Benton, the town and county where President Kennedy flew over!" Wow! I can see the tourism boom!

One Benton fact that is not in the book (because the book was written in 1964) I want to mention. George Harrison visited Benton, Illinois before the Beatles were famous in the USA. His sister lived in Benton, and he stayed with her for one month. The radio station interviewed him and they played a record and introduced it as a song from a group from Europe. WFRX is credited as the first radio station in America to play a Beatles song. The house he stayed in is now a bed and breakfast called "Hard Day's Night." Yes, folks, I did not make that up. A national radio station reported the story in the summer of 1999. The Today Show did a story on this in 2000.

So, if you get a chance you may want to visit Benton, Illinois in Franklin County. The town is located off of U.S. Route 57. Tell them Gordon sent you!

P.S. You will read a lot more about Benton in later stories in this book, so beware.

London, England
"Oh, How Different"

In 1985, I visited London for the first time. I was so excited. When you first arrive in England, you think that it will be easy to get around and communicate because they are supposed to speak the same language. I don't know what happened when our ancestors left England for the New World, but they must have left something behind. Take it from me; they don't speak the same language! They have different words for everything!

One of the most unusual things you see are cars driving on the "wrong" side of the road. That was confusing enough. And the cars were all so small, and they all drove so fast. In fact, I later learned that speed limits are almost non-existent throughout Europe. You walk across the street and almost get run over. I can't believe how fast those people drove in town!

Another thing, they talk different. I kind of liked the accent, but half the time I don't know what the world they are talking about. In Scotland they talk so fast it is impossible to understand them, without saying, "What?" I was totally lost there.

When you order food from the menu, you may want to ask first. For example, don't ask for "French fries," because in England French fries are "chips." I guess they don't want to give the French credit for anything. I think there is a big feud going on between the French and the English. I don't know what they actually call potato chips?

When I was riding the train from the airport to downtown London, I wanted to go to the restroom. I walked down the hall looking for it, but I couldn't find it anywhere. Finally, I asked, and the attendant said it was down the hall to the right. I went down the hall, and all I saw was a room with a sign "WC" on it. WC? What in the heck is that? I found out that it stood for "Water Closet," and yes, it was the bathroom.

A friend who is a native of England once told me that one day in the British Parliament, they wanted to put the initials of all the Parliament members on the doors outside their offices. Winston Churchill, who was a Parliament member at the time, quickly got up from his seat and said, "I object!"

When using the bathroom, the sign would say, "exposed," and that meant that someone was using it, don't go in! I guess this means that if someone walks in on you, you get "exposed."

And the sex thing–there were no men and women bathrooms, just one. At one facility that was unisex, you go in, an attendant hands you a few sheets of folded toilet paper, you pay about 25 cents, and then go into a stall. Oh, how awful! What if you needed more paper, what would you do? And what if you had no money?

Another favorite story I once heard has to do with a debate Sir Winston Churchill was having on the floor of Parliament with a lady member. The lady member of Parliament got kind of nasty and launch out at

Churchill. "If I was your wife, I would put poison in your coffee," she said. Sir Winston, not wanting anyone else to get the last word, replied, "If I was your husband, I would drink it!"

Speaking of politics, I once heard the story (original author unknown) of a little old lady in England who was voting for the first time when women were give the right to vote. She got up early, put on her best dress, her lip stick, and spent an hour on her hair, wanting to look just right. (What is it about women and their hair? It takes a guy 15 minutes to get ready and a woman not less than an hour. What do they do in that bathroom? I guess that will always be their great secret!)

Well, back to the story. The sweet little old British lady was excited. Her son picked her up and brought her to the polls. Finally, after spending a long time in the voting booth, the little old lady came out. Her son could tell right away that she was disappointed.

On the ride home, the son said, "Mother, who did you vote for?" The lady said, "Well, Son, I looked on the ballot and read the names of the candidates, the names of such great people running for the offices, such find noble people. I just couldn't find it in my heart to vote against any of them. So, I just wrote on the bottom of the ballot, 'God Bless You All.'"

KIDS
"THEY SAY THE CRAZIEST THINGS!"

Aren't kids something? The younger they are the truthful they are. They don't learn to lie until they get a little older. The younger the children are the more honest, sometimes too honest. Have you ever gone to a restaurant where kids under 6 eat free? Your kid just turned 6, and you tell them to say that they are 5, in order to save five bucks. What do they say? The cashier looks the kid in the eyes and says, "How old are you honey?" The parents wait with great anticipation, the suspense is high. The kid says, "My mommy told me to say 5, but I turned 6 last week."

Another thing about kids, they always ask the funniest questions. They drive the parents crazy asking, "Why?" "Why?" "How come?" etc. My wife used to teach Sunday school for five-year-olds. She was giving a lesson on the power of God. One of the kids was so taken up by the lesson, he asked, "Is God more powerful than Mighty Mouse?" If He is, than He must be awful powerful!

I once overheard a little boy talking to his dad in the store. The dad was trying to get his wife and son to hurry up. The dad said, "I have to go back to work." The little boy asked, "Why?" The dad replied, "So I can make money." The little boy said, "So I can buy more toys?"

When my wife was pregnant, our friends Mark and Diane Novak's little girl Christina was fascinated by the size of her belly. Every time she came over she would look at her belly and say, "There's a baby in there!" We all thought that was very funny, until one day Christina was at the grocery store. While there she saw a large older woman, went up to her, pointed at her belly and said, "Is there a baby in there?" The woman responded, "No, honey, I'm just fat!"

THE WEATHER MAN
"I CAN'T BELIEVE I'M ON TV!"

Don't you just love the people who do the weather on local TV stations? Where do these TV stations get these people? They are usually people who can't make it as an anchorman, but settle for the weather. They get up there, day after day, read this stuff from the National Weather Service, and act like they are experts. You should see our local TV weatherman. When he does the weather, our anchorman gives him credit when we have good weather and gives him crap when the weather is bad. He says, "Thanks for a great forecast!" or, "Be nice to us today." They act like the weatherman is responsible for the weather.

If the truth was known, I believe the weatherman really prays for bad weather. Their ideal day is when we are under a storm warning. They put on their best suit, and they are "king for the day." They go on the news first; the big story is the weather. They interrupt the broadcast, every chance they get, to discuss the weather. And don't you just love it, they always do it right when the show you're watching is getting good, we are finally getting to the punch line, and there's the smiley face of our local weatherman. I think they watch the TV and do it for spite. I can see them say, "Let's wait until the punch line and then let's interrupt." The weatherman gets so excited; he's finally in the spotlight; all the attention is focused on the weatherman. He has finally arrived!

And do these weathermen exaggerate! Yes, every chance they get. There may be a slight chance for a tornado or a thunderstorm. They say, "Take Cover!" they go on and on, they tell you where you should be when the tornado hits, "Run to the ditch! Go to the basement!" I often wonder, if it really was a big risk and we all should really take cover, why is he still on the air? Why is he not taking cover? So, my motto is not to get too excited until the TV station goes off the air. When he is not there, then it's time to go to the basement!

My San Diego Trip
"Never Travel with Two Women"

In 1999 I attended a conference for the American Association of Motor Vehicle Administrators in San Diego, California. I had attended several conferences in the past, however, this time I was to travel with two ladies from my office, Sherry Mansker and LeeAnn Sproul. Neither of the two ladies had been to San Diego before and I had been there three times. I guess they saw me as an "expert" and they used and abused me as their personal tour guide and chauffeur. We rented a car and I was the one that was asked to drive them all over San Diego after our meetings in the afternoon and evening. Don't you feel sorry for me?

Even though I was actually younger than the two gals, I kind of ended up as their guardian as well. I would try to get them to go to their rooms at a reasonable hour so they could get up in the morning for our meetings. However, each morning they were always on time, but they seemed extra tired. I could not figure this out, until one night I caught them. I had dropped them off, after a drive, to go to their room. Like little school girls they waited until I had gone down the hall to my room. I fooled them and went the other direction. They went to the lounge. Their faces turned red when I walked into the lounge to see them sitting at a table drinking. I found out later that they had been there the night before until the place closed at 3 A.M.

I am a non-smoker and can't figure out those who smoke. And these two gals smoked cigarettes. Not only do they smoke, but they have to have a specific brand and type of cigarettes. In my mind, a smoke is a smoke, but not for these gals. One day I drove them all over San Diego hunting for a specific type of cigarettes. We finally found them in a tobacco store 45 minutes later!

One evening Sherry and LeeAnn went out about town without an escort. (Yes, I got tired of being their baby-sitter.) And yes, they got in trouble! They thought it would be fun to go on a horse and buggy ride. They road for a few minutes when all of a sudden the horse started to act up. The horse jumped and then stopped real fast, LeeAnn actually fell out of the carriage, and then the horse started running out of control. Sherry had the scare of her life. When the driver got the horse to stop, Sherry yelled to the driver, "Get me out of here! This is the worst damn buggy ride I ever had! And I'm not paying!" She then jumped out of the buggy and ran down the street with the driver yelling, "You didn't pay! You didn't pay!"

When they finally told me this story, I spent the rest of the trip trying to avoid the police, in case the driver had turned the ladies in.

When I finally made it back home to my wife, I was really glad to see her. I almost didn't survive those five days in San Diego! I told my wife about all the things that happened, and then I decided to play a joke on her. I told her that I liked everything about my room, but I had a hard time trying to sleep because the ladies snored too loud. My wife's eyes almost popped out of her head. "You stayed in the same room!!" she yelled.

"No, just kidding." She didn't think that was funny.

POLITICS
"THE ART OF RIDING THE FENCE"

Isn't it interesting that politicians want to be for things no one can be against? And they are strongly against things everyone is against. They try to "commercialize" their offices and their profession. Everything they do or say is like a commercial. The politician is now the product. And products are "all things to all people."

Once Barry Goldwater was asked where he stood on segregation, and he jokingly answered, "Where are you from?"

I once personally spoke to one of the most liberal Senators in the U.S. Senate. Knowing I was conservative, he had the nerve to say that he was "conservative" on fiscal issues. He wanted even me to like him. I think that politicians have to be people who spend their entire lives seeking approval. Many of them probably spend their entire childhoods never pleasing their parents. So, we, the general public and the voters, have to spend our lives giving the politician our "stamp of approval" by voting for them on election day, and by giving them the "thumbs up" when the pollster calls taking the latest public opinion survey.

I heard one politician at an after dinner speech many years ago mention these "Four Golden Rules of Politics." The first was, "Never buy your ticket until you hear the train whistle." By this rule, he meant only go with the sure things in life. The second rule was,

"Always be strong for something that no one can be against." This one is my favorite. In campaigns you will see candidates using this rule all the time. The third was, "Never use one word, if three will do." People in government like to hear themselves talk. The more they say, the more important they look. That is what gets votes. The fourth rule was, "Always stick to your party. If it is in trouble, try to save it, but if it sinks, go down with the ship." These rules were written probably in the 1940s when political loyalty was a big deal. Today, with politicians changing political parties right and left, I doubt if rule number four would hold up today. Nevertheless, I really thought these rules were funny and even though I heard them probably 25 years ago, to this day I recall them from memory.

CHAPTER 2

BRIGHTEN YOUR DAY WITH "THE FAMILY"

Every morning when we get out of bed, most of us have to deal with "The Family." Why not have some fun with our family members and remember some of the funny stories you heard over the years.

I hope the stories from my family will help brighten your day, start it out with a laugh, and motivate you to think about the funny stories that have occurred in your own family.

After all, you have plenty of time to think, while you are in that special room, doing your business.

THE MAILMAN
"I JUST LOVE YOUR POSTCARDS"

I've got to tell you about my parents' mailman in Benton. It's probably the only place in America where the mailman rings your doorbell, says hello, and tells you what type of mail you have. For example, when I was home (I couldn't help but think that Norman Rockwell would have loved this picture), the doorbell rang (we could see the mailman from the kitchen window), and both of my parents rushed to the door to greet him. After the warm greeting, the mailman told my dad in an anxious way, "Oh, Jack, you got some checks!"

Then, my parents laughed a little and called me to the door to introduce me to the mailman. "This is our son, Gordon, from Springfield." I had to shake the mailman's hand as if he were a long lost friend. The mailman's response to me was, "You must be the one who travels so much. I just love your postcards!"

About two weeks earlier, my dad's cousin was dropping my great aunt off at her house, when he put his car in reverse by mistake. The car went into the ditch. He was so embarrassed he swore my aunt to secrecy. However, he didn't know that our friendly mailman was in the neighborhood. Before my dad's cousin had made it home (and Benton is one of those towns that it takes less than five minutes to drive anywhere), he had three messages on his machine asking if he was OK.

THE SALTY POTATOES
"DISHES ANYONE?"

My aunt is very sensitive about her cooking. She would often get very mad at her relatives when they complained about it. If she labored all day in the kitchen, she surely didn't deserve complaints. In fact, on one particular day, my aunt got mad and told her family that the next time anyone complained about her cooking, they would have to do the dishes. Well, later in the meal, my dad took a bite of the potatoes, and said, "Boy, are these potatoes salty!" There was complete silence, while everyone stared at my aunt and my dad. My dad, realizing what he had said, quickly added, "But, that's the way I like them!"

MY GRANDMOTHER
"A SPECIAL LADY"

My grandmother, Loretta Rusher, was a special lady. However, she was very hard headed and had some strange ideas. She was always very protective of her kids when they were growing up. My mother was terrified of water and she never learned how to swim. In fact, her mother told her, "Never get into the water until you learn how to swim!" I guess I followed her advice too, and to this day I can't swim either.

When I was a kid, I often asked my grandmother about her advice on swimming, and she just would never admit that it didn't make any sense. I would say, "Grandmother, how can you learn how to swim without getting into the water?" Her response was, "You know you could drown! Don't you dare, get into that water! After you learn how to swim, you can spend as much time in the water that you would like!" I finally gave up trying to talk any sense into her on that subject.

She also had some odd behaviors as well as her own dictionary. When you stayed over night, she would always ask you if you would like to have "a toast" for breakfast. Not "toast," but always "a toast."

When she would see someone she knew at the grocery store, they had to speak to her first. I remember on several occasions she would say, "I saw (so and so) in the store today and she didn't even speak to me!" I would often ask her, "Did you speak to them,

Grandma?" And she would say, "I'm not going to speak to them unless they speak to me!" If everyone were like that, then we would have a quiet world. I could never get her to understand that. I think because of my grandma, I always make a point to speak first when I run into anyone.

She was extra clean and always wiped everything with her towel. I can see her now, standing in the kitchen with her towel over her shoulder. You would take a shower, and the minute you stepped out of the bathroom she would be in there wiping the bathroom walls down. She would be in there for an hour wiping the shower and shining the fixtures. I believe her bathroom was clean enough to eat dinner off of.

I remember how much my grandma complained when one of my uncles took a shower over at her house. She told me that he got "water all over the shower." I asked her, "How can you take a shower without getting water on it?" Her response was, "I don't when I take a shower." She would never explain this to me, but she must have made a major discovery–how to take a shower with no water!

When I moved away to college, she would write me letters. In the letters, she would never say much, except what happened that day. She would say that she got up at 6 A.M., ate breakfast, waited for the mailman to come (yes, mailmen are quite popular in Benton.) She would tell me what she got in the mail, and funny things other relatives would say. She would always write "Ha, Ha" after a funny remark. Then she would write, "I have to go now and mail this letter."

It was fun to get a letter from my grandma.

ROUTINES
"DO IT TODAY . . . OR DIE!"

Isn't it something that we all get into certain routines? Some people are so strongly entrenched that only death will keep them from doing certain things.

My Grandmother Rusher was one of those people. When her social security check came, the first Tuesday of each month, she had to go to the bank that morning, cash her check, pay each of her bills by cash, and then she would go home. This was an all day project. The check would come around 10 A.M., and if the mailman was late, she would call the post office. She would walk up town and go to the bank and cash her check, then to Western Auto to pay her monthly bill on her furniture, then to the power company, then to the phone company.

In her small town, all of these places were within walking distance. Now if it rained or if the weather was bad, my mother would take her in the car. She wouldn't dare send payment for her bills in the mail through the post office. "You can't trust those people," she would often say. "They may lose your money, and then what?"

One cold and icy winter day, the schools were closed for the snow. It was the first Tuesday of the month, and her social security check came. My grandmother called my mom to take her on her errands. My mother told her to wait until the weather cleared up, because it was real bad. My grandmother would not wait. What if they turned her electricity off, or came to pick up her furniture? She had to pay her bills, and she had to pay them today! My mother finally agreed to take her. My mother tried to get out of the driveway but the snow was too deep. My dad helped her clean off the ice and snow, and it took her about 45 minutes to get to my grandmother's house. When my mother got there, my grandmother was gone. My mother finally found her walking down the road to town with her boots and heavy coat on. She just had to pay those bills; she couldn't wait any longer!

GRANDMA WAYMAN
"HER VIEW OF TELEVISION"

My grandmother on the other side of the family was quite a character as well. Her name was Gertrude Wayman. First of all, her first name gets your attention because people do not name babies Gertrude any more. When Charlotte was pregnant I would often get the question, "What will you name the baby?" I would respond with a serious look, "Gertrude." It was really fun to see people's reaction. Most of the people would just stare, too shocked to respond. I would then follow with the statement, "My grandmother was named Gertrude and I was real close to her and promised my family that if I ever had a daughter I would name her Gertrude." It is amazing how many people would say, "Oh what a nice name."

Well, Gertrude was a nice name in the 1890s when my grandmother was born. And she indeed was a nice lady. She was always friendly to everyone and never met a stranger. She would sit on her porch, living by herself at age 90, without locking her doors. She would invite perfect strangers, who may be going door to door selling things, into her house for a chat. She would buy nearly everything that was being sold because the people were "so nice."

Grandma Wayman never was corrupted by the television. In fact, she did not have a television. Her religion prevented her from having one and she really had no desire to watch it. She actually never figured out the technology. Once I was going to be on television on a news program. They had filmed me earlier that afternoon for the evening news. We picked her up and wanted her to see me. I was in the room when the news was on. She could not figure out why I was there when I was supposed to be on television. She was very confused. In her mind, everything was live.

Those were the good old days.

MY GRANDFATHER
"PLAY THE CARDS FAIR!"

My grandfather, Jesse Rusher, was quite a character as well. My biggest memory of him is all of his
coughing. When I was very young, I would hear him
just cough and cough. He smoked cigarettes that he
rolled himself. After each puff, he would cough for
two to three minutes. Then he would take another
puff. I remember asking him, "Grandpa, why do you
cough so much?" His response was, "These damn
cigarettes!" I must have been only eight or nine
years old, when I asked him, "Why do you smoke
then?" He just shook his head and said, "Hell, I don't
know!" To this day, I am convinced that I never took
one puff of a cigarette because of that question and
that cough.

I also remember him talking about the depression.
Once he said, "The depression would not have been
nearly as bad, if it didn't come right in the middle
of hard times." I always thought that was funny, but
true. He was always poor and never had much, but
he always had a good time. He enjoyed a good laugh
and telling jokes. I may have got my sense of humor
from him.

He was quite a card player. My grandparents would
play cards with their neighbors, the Reeds. The men
would partner with one another. They would win
every game because they would cheat. And, the
women could never figure out why they always lost.

Sometimes the final score would be 105 to 15 and the women would complain about how bad they did. My grandfather would say, "I think you did pretty good!"

They had card signals, hand signals and verbal signals for every situation one could imagine. I would get such a kick out of watching them. When my grandfather wanted spades, he would talk about doing some gardening in the yard. When he was going diamonds, he would talk about jewelry. They would show each others' cards when the ladies' backs were turned. They would often take cards from the deck and play them again–anything to win. Then they would look at me and just laugh. The women never new what was so funny.

He was the type that would have the nerve to say, "Play the cards fair now, I know what I dealt you!"

PARENTS
"CAN THEY FOLLOW DIRECTIONS?"

Parents, you love them, but don't they get on your nerves? When they get older, I guess, they're paying us back for all the headaches we caused them when we were kids. My dad thought he was always "right." He was even going to write a book, "How to Do Everything Right," until he found out someone else had written one with the same title. I couldn't tell him anything, even something simple, like directions to my new house.

As you know by now, my parents are from, what town? Benton. I currently live in Springfield, a city about three hours away. For them to come visit was a major thing, since they hardly ever traveled. So, when I bought a new house, they were very nervous on the directions. I drew out everything on a map, with detailed instructions. Before they left, I even called them on the phone. I said, "When you're coming into town, you stay on Route 55 until you get to Exit 94, where you exit at East Lake Drive. Stay on 55 North," I said, "in the right lane that says Chicago. Whatever you do, do not go into Springfield. Stay in the right lane, stay right, until you turn on Exit 94."

What did they do? They went left. As soon as they got into town, they went straight into Springfield and did not stay right. They called me and said that they were lost. I asked them, "Why didn't you follow my directions, stay in the right lane that said 'Chicago North'?" Their response was, "You live in Springfield, not Chicago!"

DRUGS IN BENTON
"MY MOM IN THE MIDDLE"

My small home town of Benton is about 35 miles away from Carbondale, Illinois–home of Southern Illinois University. I think because of the proximity of the university and the fact that Benton has a small airport, the town has experienced a lot of drug activity. Some have called Benton the "drug capital of Southern Illinois."

A few years ago my mother was on her way home to find her street blocked off. There were FBI agents everywhere, there was the SWAT team and there was a helicopter hovering over the street. It looked like something you would see in the movies. She later found out that there was a big drug bust on her street. One of her neighbors was a big drug dealer. It was one of the biggest drug busts in the state.

On another occasion, my mother kept seeing these kids hanging out by a building in her back yard. This went on for several nights. It seemed like they were moving around rocks by the building. After she called the police, they discovered that they were using my mother's back yard as a drop off place for drugs. Money would be placed under a rock by the buyer and the seller would later pick up the money, place the drugs under the rock, and the buyer would come back to get the drugs. My poor mom!

Jay Leno mentioned a Benton drug story in his monologue on the Tonight Show a few years ago. It was another drug bust. There was quite a sophisticated operation going on. What would happen is if you wanted drugs, you would call the local pizza establishment, and mention you wanted a certain type of pizza. That would be the code for drugs. They would actually deliver the drugs directly to your home in a pizza box!

Only in Benton!

CHAPTER 3

MOTIVATE YOUR DAY

We all need to have things that will help motivate us to get through the day, to do a better job, to reach for the stars. These stories are to be read, when part of you wants to laugh and the other parts wants to think. The following accounts have deep messages, but will still make you laugh. Please pay close attention and read between the lines. (You do not have to read backwards, or place the book in front of the mirror to read a secret message, just read and think!)

The Difference Between a Malt and a Shake
"One Cherry or Two?"

How much does an employee need to know? How extensive should a new employee's orientation be? How much cross training is necessary in the work place?

Decisions relating to training are very important to management. Although training is expensive, it is an investment in the organization. Employees have a basic human need to understand the "why" aspects of their jobs. Supervisors who do not take the time to teach their employees why things are the way they are, run the risk of having robotic employees who do not think for themselves.

The following true story illustrates the importance of training and teaching the employees the reason why.

The Difference between a Malt and a Shake

It all happened one Sunday after church services when I went to Steak 'N Shake with friends for lunch in Springfield. We were greeted by a beautiful waitress who took our order. After a few minutes it was obvious that our waitress was a new employee for the restaurant. When it was my turn to order, I selected my usual steak burger with a chocolate malt. However, this time by mistake I ordered a chocolate "shake" instead of a "malt."

I always liked the malt flavor and these days it's hard to find a restaurant that offers both shakes and malts.

After the waitress had completed taking the orders for our table, I remembered that I had said "shake" instead of "malt." I asked the waitress to change my order.

She responded, "Oh, that's ok, the only difference between a malt and a shake is that the malt has two cherries and the shake has one." I was dumbfounded. Everyone at our table looked at each other in amazement. I went on to disagree with the waitress. I explained that there was a major difference. Malts, I said, have a malted powder that changes the taste.

She continued to disagree and said that the lady behind the counter who makes the ice cream items told her that the malts had two cherries and the shakes had one. The waitress felt so strongly about her point that I had to get the manager to prove that she was wrong. Her final response was, "I always thought that was kind of silly."

The point of this story is that it is important for management to explain "why" things are done the way they are done. I do not blame the waitress for not knowing the difference between a shake and a malt. The supervisor only told her what she "needed to know." She was told that in order to distinguish between the two, one cherry was placed in the shakes while two cherries were placed in the malts. Although this was important, the reason "why" was not explained to the waitress.

In management it is important to explain "why." If we fail to do this, we will have employees who do not know the difference between a malt and a shake.

Well, that's the serious part of this book; let's get back to the funny stuff.

PERCEPTION IS EVERYTHING
"THE BIGGEST BUILDING IN THE WORLD"

The biggest city around Benton is Carbondale, with a population of 35,000. The people in Benton really get excited when big things happen in the area. For example, my grandmother always told the story about when they built "The Wood Building." It was in the 1930s when big buildings were a rarity, especially in Southern Illinois. She said that people came from miles around just to watch them build this huge building on the public square. They would watch for hours as the cranes lifted the blocks and frames up to build this huge skyscraper. I asked my grandmother, "How many stories did the Wood Building have?" She said, "Six!" Well, to my grandmother, the Wood Building was the tallest building in the world. Nothing could be bigger.

As the years went by, my grandmother always compared everything in size to the Wood Building. In the late 1970s, my family went to Chicago, and my grandmother went there for the first time. I don't think she had ever been out of the county prior to that trip. She was quite taken in with all the buildings and the people. We took her to the Sears Tower, and when we were in the elevator going up to the 110th floor, she leaned over to my mother and asked, as serious as she could, "Is this building taller than the Wood Building?" Well, in the mind of my grandmother, the Wood Building was the tallest building in the world! So move over Sears Tower!

MY SPECIAL LONDON FRIEND
"OH, WHAT A DIFFERENT WORLD"

In 1990, I went to London for the second time. I had enjoyed the city so much, I just had to go back. This time, my traveling companion backed out at the last moment, so I decided to go alone.

During both of my trips, I stayed at hostels. These are like college dorms, no-thrill, cheap hotels. In fact, the one in London charged only $20 per day, which included two meals. Heck, I spent more than $20 per day living in Springfield!

One of the neat things about staying at a hostel is that you meet people from all over the world. Traveling alone especially made it interesting because singles would share rooms with 2 or 3 other people.

During my stay I had several different roommates. On the day before I was scheduled to leave London, I returned to my room to find a new roommate. I concluded right away that this guy was not your ordinary tourist. In fact, his name was Karimu, and he was from a small village in West Africa. This was his first visit to a modern society. He had just arrived. He was staying in the hostel for a few days before he began his task of learning English to study the Bible. He was going to be a missionary for a Christian church.

When I walked into the room, he was laying on the bed dressed in a polyester suit, shivering. I thought that was unusual, because I was not at all cold, it was about 75 degrees outside. After introducing myself, I asked him, since he was so cold, why wasn't he covering up with the blankets on the bed? He did not understand. He had never covered up with blankets in a bed before.

In his country the temperature was over 100 degrees every day, all the time. In the winter, he later told me, the temperature got down to around 80 degrees and everyone would stop work and gather around a fire until it got warmer! (This is true, ladies and gentlemen. I'm not making this up!) So, for 75 degrees, it was cold!

I explained to him what the blankets were and that you could pull them down and get under them to stay warm. He was quite taken in by this, and really liked the idea. Just think, placing cotton or wool over your body to get warm, now that's an idea!

In his village, he lived in a room with his entire family. They all slept on the floor together (his brothers and sisters, their wives, and their grandparents.) They had no beds, and especially no blankets. What a way to live. I guess there was no where to go in private to tell mother-in-law jokes.

He told me that he would go for miles by donkey to the general store to buy supplies. If he wanted to buy items there were no selections or choices to make. For example, if he wanted socks, there would be only one kind; soap, one kind; etc. So, when I took him shopping in London, he was amazed.

In fact, on our way to the shops, he had never been in an automobile before, so we took a cab. I will never forget the facial expression when he was riding in that car. He was so proud. He thought only rich people road in cars. He had finally arrived.

When arriving at one shop, he couldn't get over what he called "the moving steps"–the escalator. He asked, "How can steps move?" Again, his eyes almost popped out of his head. Just think, steps that actually moved. I can see him trying to describe this to his family back home in Africa!

His biggest fascination was a store that only sold socks. He just stood there and stared at the socks. He couldn't believe that they had so many different pairs of socks. He would have spent hours there if I hadn't pushed him out of the store.

I really enjoyed being his tour guide for my last two days in London. When I was about to depart, I had this wet towel. (In a hostel, you bring your towel with you.) However, I did not want to pack a wet towel to take home. I was about ready to throw it away, when I thought that maybe Karimu would like it. Since, he was so poor and didn't have much, I asked him. He was so excited about that towel; it was like I had given him a new car! He said, "Yes! Yes!" and thanked me about twenty times.

A few months later, I got a letter from Karimu. In the letter he explained why he was so excited about the towel. This is what he said:

· · · · · · ·

"I still have the towel you gave me just when you were about to leave. That was something very important in my custom back home in West Africa–Sierra. Leaving anything on departure with a friend, especially something used personally is clear manifestation of sincere friendship and love. Because our customs and tradition vary so much, I have thought it fit to tell you."

• • • • • • •

So now I understood. Later on in his letter, he stated that he would "keep the towel forever."

Well, there is nothing funny I can say about that. I now understood. Karimu was a special guy. I will never forget him.

THE SALARY GAME
"HOW MUCH DO YOU MAKE?"

The other day I went to the United States Post Office and bought some stamps. At our post office, we have "The Stamp Store," a spot in the post office where all they do is sell stamps. They have any kind of stamp you can image. "What kind of stamp would you like, sir? Would that be one with Superman on it, President Nixon, or the flag?" Decisions, Decisions.

That afternoon, I saw the same guy that sold me stamps in line at a fast food restaurant waiting for hamburgers. The lady behind the counter said, "How may I help you? Would you like a small hamburger, a medium size, or an extra large?"

Who decides on how much someone makes? How come the lady behind the hamburger counter makes about $6 per hour with no benefits, while the guy selling stamps makes $20 per hour, health benefits, retirement, vacation, etc.?

The guy that counts out your pills in the pharmacy makes at least $100 per hour and the guy who counts your tomatoes in the grocery store makes around $6. Did you ever think about how these decisions were made? At one time in our history, someone or something had to decide on how much a certain task is worth. Is there a wizard that says someone who counts pills makes more than someone who counts tomatoes? That someone who sells stamps makes more than someone whom sells hamburgers?

Can you imagine trying to explain this to someone from another planet? Well, I just don't know. It doesn't make sense, but it is what makes our free enterprise system work. You get paid as much as you can get away with. If you can convince someone that your job is worthy of a big salary, you will achieve it. Now you know why everyone from around the world wants to come to America!

THE DOCTOR'S OFFICE
"WHAT AN EXPERIENCE"

Don't you just love it when you're sick, you call the doctor's office and ask for a prescription over the phone, and they make you come into the office? One day when I was sick, I called the doctor's office and asked to talk to the nurse. She asked me to list my symptoms. I told her I had the flu and needed an antibiotic. She went on to say, "Do you have a temperature? Do you feel achy?" etc., etc. I answered all her questions, and then the nurse said, "Hold on." A few minutes later, she came back to the phone, and said that the doctor wanted to see me.

The doctor wanted to see me? Boy, did I feel special. I was sick; all I needed was an antibiotic. I had the flu, and the doctor wanted to see me! I can't figure out their racket. Sometimes, I can call in and get a prescription over the phone, while other times I have to come in. I had the same symptoms that I had had previously, but this time I had to come into the office to see the doctor.

I believe they must have a quota on the number of patients the doctor has to see per day. Instead of asking the doctor, all the nurse really did was look at the appointment book. Does the doctor have 50 patients with appointments today or 40? If he has 40, ten more people have to come in. After the 50th patient, the nurse can start writing prescriptions over the phone.

What I would like to do is figure out when the best time of day to call into the office would be. I think it has to be late in the afternoon, right before the doctor goes home, on a day before his day off. Then, I'm sure one could get a prescription over the phone.

On that day, I finally make it to the doctor. When I first get there I have to wait in the waiting room for a good 30 to 45 minutes if I'm lucky (my wife has to wait two hours to see her doctor). And doctors love for people to wait. (That's why they call it the waiting room.) If you're not sick when you go in, you're bound to catch something in the waiting room. There are people couching, hacking, and breathing all over you, how awful!

They finally call my name. I make it to the second room. Before I go into the second room, the nurse stops and weighs me. Here I have the flu, and the doctor wants to know how much I weigh. How is that relevant? Then, she closes the door and I wait some more. A few minutes later, the nurse comes in and takes my temperature and my blood pressure. I have the flu, why is she taking my blood pressure? I guess they have to do it to everyone, so we will feel like we're getting our money's worth.

She asks me all the same questions she did over the phone. I answer them again. She then tells me to get undress and put this silly robe on. She leaves and says the doctor will be with me "shortly." I don't know what her definition of "shortly" was, but it's certainly not the same as mine. I sit there and sit there freezing to death with this robe on. It looked like she would realize that freezing does not help someone with the flu. Finally, about 30 minutes later, the doctor came in.

The doctor says, "How are you doing today?" I almost say "fine" (since we are suppose to say that when that question is asked in our society), but I realize that I am sick, so I stop myself and say, "I think I have the flu." The doctor then reads the chart and asks me the same questions again that the nurse has already asked me. Then he says, "Ok, we'll take some tests." You can't go all the way to the doctor without taking some tests. This will bring the bill to an acceptable level. He calls the nurse back in, takes some blood, asks me to urinate in a cup, and then I am asked to sit in his office.

I sit in his office staring at the pictures of his family, his credentials and all the awards he received. He probably does that on purpose, so the patients will have more confidence in his diagnosis. After all, who would question someone with all of those certificates?

I sit there for another 30 minutes. The doctor comes in, finally, and says, "It looks like you have the flu! I'll give you an antibiotic. Take this three times daily, get plenty of rest, and drink lots of liquid."

Boy, that was some work on his part! He figured out I had the flu. Wow! His years of medical training paid off! I now wasted a half a day in the doctors' office. If he had given me the antibiotic over the phone in the first place, I would have spent all day resting in bed, getting better. But, he has to make his quota! Fifty patients per day! "Next!"

THE NEUROLOGIST OFFICE
"THE VISIT"

When my wife had a seizure, we went to the emergency room. They did several thousand dollars worth of tests and she had to stay in the hospital for a 23-hour observation period. At the end of the time, the neurologist came into the room and told her that she could go home. When asked what was wrong with her, the response was, "I can tell you what you do not have." The doctor went on to say that she didn't have a brain tumor, electrical activity in the brain, etc. She said they didn't know what was wrong with her, but she was fine. I had a hard time believing she was fine because she had had a seizure and major memory loss.

Since all of her tests came back negative, the only test she had not had was a neuro-psychological evaluation test. This test, which cost over $1,000, involved over three hours of questions. She was asked to read stuff and reflect on it, to look at pictures, etc. The test took 30 days to get the results. We made an appointment with the doctor to discuss the results. When asked what the results were, the doctor said that the results indicated that Charlotte had a memory problem.

She has a memory problem? We paid $1,000 for a doctor to acknowledge that Charlotte had a memory problem? That was the reason for the exam in the first place. Some times I think the doctors have a racket going with all of the tests.

Our next appointment with the neurologist was also interesting. Charlotte's doctor was connected with a medical school so a resident would always come in before the "real" doctor. This resident came in first and asked, "What can I do for you?" Well, I thought, maybe tell me what the heck is going on with my wife. He seemed to know nothing about her case and spent most of his time ranging through her file that was about 100 pages long.

He asked what problems Charlotte was having. One of the problems she mentioned was she had a hard time sleeping. The doctor responded that people should not watch TV, read or use the computer two hours before bedtime. What? I thought. What in the heck would we do, just sit in a chair and stair at each other for two hours each night?

He also said that the bed should only be used for sleeping. We should not read or watch TV there. When we go to bed, our bodies should only think of sleep. I guess the poor resident didn't know much about how babies were conceived. Maybe he missed the part on reproduction in medical school!

It's a wonder how some doctors can sit there and talk with a straight face. These doctors told us nothing that was useful. They just confirmed her symptoms and said, "Nothing is wrong." And, of course, they then give us a big bill.

THE ANNIVERSARY DINNER
"HOW DID THAT HAPPEN?"

This next story is very amazing and you may think I am exaggerating or not telling the truth. I would understand you thinking this way, but it is nothing but the truth, the absolute truth.

There was a restaurant, called Mountain Jacks, that I used to eat at on a regular basis for lunch. The prices were reasonable for lunch for such a nice and fancy restaurant. However, in the evening the menu would change and the prices would go out of the roof. People would go there for special occasions to celebrate birthdays and anniversaries.

The tables all had bottles of wine on them, with fancy tags that identified the type of wine. One day, I was having lunch with a friend, and he was showing me a fancy new pen he had purchased. I wanted to write with it, so I took the tag on the bottle, turned it over and wrote, "Best Wishes, Gordon Wayman."

A few weeks later, some friends of mine, Dr. Bob Wenneborg and his wife Carolyn, got me aside after church and said, "Thank you so much for the bottle of wine!" The doctor said, "But, how did you know we were going to celebrate our anniversary at Mountain Jacks?"

What are the odds of my signed tag on the wine staying on the table for several weeks without being spotted? What are the odds of the wine not being purchased? What are the odds of my friends eating at that specific restaurant? What are the odds of them being seated at the same table that I sat at several weeks earlier? What are the odds of them looking at the other side of the tag?

You do the math!

POLITICS
"THE SELLING OF THE CANDIDATES"

"Politics" is defined as the "art or science of political government" (The American Heritage Dictionary). I often wondered if it was a coincidence that the word "Politics" ends with the word "tics." A "tick" is defined as a "bloodsucking parasitic arachnids or louse like insect" (The American Heritage Dictionary). So, it shouldn't surprise us when there is so much blood sucking going on in political campaigns today.

Politicians are always out for blood. They spend every breathing hour of every day trying to get their names in the papers and their faces on television. They have to do it, because they are always running for re-election or for higher office. The political campaigns today are conducted the same way big corporations sell soap and beer. The largest portion of the campaign's budget is spent on television commercials. The candidate is "sold" like soap.

A few years ago, a guy named Raymond Poe (I understand he is a real nice guy and I am not mentioning his story to be critical) was running for State Representative in the Springfield, Illinois area for the first time. My wife and I would often joke about his campaign slogans. These days to run for office, you have to have a slogan, something for people to remember you by. And, his slogan was "Poe Cares–Think Poe." I thought that was a clever slogan. It showed that the candidate cared about people, and it also told people to think. After all, we would need to think in order to remember the name of the candidate, wouldn't we? So, thinking Poe would allow us to remember his name when we went into the voting booth. How clever. It must have worked, because Poe won.

Two years later, Mr. Poe ran for re-election. His slogan changed to, "Elect Poe, He's Just Like Us." Now, I just did not like the new slogan. My wife couldn't figure out why he changed his slogan. "Poe Cares" got him elected, why couldn't it get him re-elected? I would much rather have someone who "cares," instead of someone who is like everyone else. His new slogan, "He's Just Like Us," just did not make sense. Most people don't care about others. So, the only thing I could figure out was that he cared *before* he ran for office, but now, after he got elected, he became like everyone else, careless and selfish!

That's politics!

P.S. No offense, Mr. Poe. I am sure you are a nice guy. Now he is running for Lieutenant Governor of Illinois. Good Luck!

CHAPTER 4

THINK OF THE GOOD OLD DAYS

What better way to pass the time away while on the can than to think of the good old days? We all have funny things that happened to us in the past. Think of when you were a child, when you went to school, or whenever. These thoughts always bring back laughs.

THE JERRY FALWELL STORY
"MISTAKEN FOR AN ASSASSIN"

Well, do I seem like the kind of person who would be mistaken for an assassin? When I was in college, I almost got killed in the "line of fire."

It all started at Southern Illinois University in Carbondale, Illinois. I was active in politics. I was even the president of the SIU College Republicans. Jerry Falwell, the TV minister from the Old Time Gospel Hour, was at that time president of a political organization called, "The Moral Majority." He was very well known and very controversial. He was scheduled to be on campus and speak at a dinner. A local business group sponsored the event.

One of the sponsors was a friend of mine and gave me a ticket. I had plans to attend the 7 P.M. event. However, that afternoon I was in the student center study lounge on the second floor reading. Jerry Falwell had arrived on campus early and was on the same floor doing various interviews with the press. Outside the student center were hundreds of liberal, left wing groups demonstrating against Falwell and his organization. In fact, I learned later that there were even threats against his life.

Around 5 P.M. I left the study lounge to go to my apartment to change clothes for the event that evening. While I was leaving, I walked down the hall, and to my surprise, Jerry Falwell was coming right at me. He was surrounded by a group of bodyguards followed by several others. I thought that this was my opportunity to promote our SIU College Republican Club. We had these buttons, like the old time political campaign buttons, that said "SIU College Republicans."

So, as Mr. Falwell was approaching, I reached into my jacket pocket to pull out a button to give him. Yes, you guessed it. His bodyguard thought that I was pulling out a gun from my pocket. One of the guards, about 6 feet tall and over 200 pounds, knocked me down, pulled out his gun, and Jerry Falwell was rushed to the next room. I was pushed and I slid on the floor a good six feet. A gun was in my face. My face turned three shades of red. I said, "All I wanted to do was give him this button!"

Well, the story isn't over yet. That evening shortly after I arrived to the dinner, I heard my name over the speaker system. "Would Gordon Wayman please report to the information desk in the lobby?" I thought, "What in God's name have I done now. It was only a button!" Apparently, the friend that gave me the ticket to the dinner was one of the people walking behind Jerry when the incident in the student center had occurred. He had told Jerry who I was. I was brought back stage. Mr. Falwell wanted to meet me and apologize for the actions of his security guards.

Mr. Falwell was real nice about the whole thing. He even gave me a nice gift, a "Jesus First" gold lapel pen, which I have to this day. We chatted for a couple of minutes, and I gave him my SIU College Republican button, which I am sure he does *not* have to this day.

After the dinner and speech, Mr. Falwell worked the crowd and shook hands with people by table. I was sitting with a group of friends, however, I had not had time to tell them about the incident. When Falwell came to our table, he patted me on the back and said, "Gordon, my Republican friend!" My friends looked at me with big eyes and said, "Do you know Jerry Falwell?" I said, "Oh, we go way back!"

RUNNING A CAMPAIGN
"THE FLIGHT OF MY LIFE!"

In 1982, I had the opportunity to take a leave of absence from my job with the Secretary of State and work as the campaign manager for Miki Cooper. Miki was running for State Representative in Southern Illinois. During the campaign, I would travel with the candidate all over her district. On occasion, we would go to Springfield (about 200 miles away) for meetings.

On one specific occasion, we received a call from the head of the House Campaign Committee. He wanted to meet with us that day. We had several other events scheduled, so the only way we could have made it was to fly in a chartered plane. I was kind of scared, because I had not flown in a small plane before. I had flown on big jets, but this plane held only four people.

Reluctantly, I agreed to go. Miki knew I was scared and thought it was so funny. Going to Springfield on the plane wasn't too bad. The plane had four seats facing each other. I just sat in my seat, looking straight at Miki and her husband Bob. I did not look out of the window. The weather was nice, so the ride was pretty smooth. Nevertheless, I was glad to make it on the ground.

Coming back that night was another story. In fact, it was one of the worst experiences in my life. We were up in the air in the middle of a thunderstorm.

There was lighting going through the plane. I learned what the word "turbulence" really meant. I was really scared!

At one point, the pilot, trying to talk to us and navigate at the same time, said, "I don't think we are going to make it . . ." and then he stopped the sentence. Miki said that my face turned totally white. My heart stopped. I felt that if the plane was going down, I might as well die right there and now with a heart attack!

However, a few minutes later, the pilot finished his statement. " . . . make it to Harrisburg; we may have to land in Marion instead." At that point, my heart started back. We did make it to Marion. When the plane landed, I kissed the ground, and had a new outlook on life in general.

Oh, what a wonderful world!

MEET SOMEBODY FAMOUS
"IT PAYS TO BE CONSISTENT"

During high school, I was an admirer of President Richard Nixon. (Warning: If you hate President Nixon you may want to skip this story!) He was president when I was growing up and I respected him. I know he did a lot of things wrong, and I don't excuse him for it. However, he did do some great things for our country, and I just liked the man. Is there a crime in that?

In fact, regardless of what you think of the man, he was one of the most dominating men in American politics in the 20th Century. He was vice president for eight years, ran for president three times, and served as president for seven years. During the last few years of his life, one survey asked what politician people would want to meet most, and I heard Nixon was at the top of the list.

In 1978, my best friend Kent Alsobrooks and I were planning a trip to California after our high school graduation. While in California, there was one thing I wanted to do, and that was to meet former President Nixon. He had resigned in 1974 and in 1978, he was in isolation. According to reports in the media, he wasn't seeing anyone except his close circle of friends.

My task was not easy. How could an average high school kid get an appointment to see a former president? First, I tried writing a letter to his office. With the letter, I poured it on strong, how I admired him, how he had influenced my life, etc. A few weeks later, I received a nice reply, regretting that President Nixon was unable to meet with me.

I didn't want to stop at that. So, I then wrote every politician I could think of including Governor Jim Thompson of Illinois, Senator Charles Percy from Illinois and several U.S. Congressmen. I asked if they would write letters on my behalf. Believe it our not, most of them did. I mean, what did they have to lose? I waited, but heard no response from Nixon's office.

I then saw Illinois Senator Percy at a political function and got him in a corner. Politicians will say anything to get a constituent off of their back! Remember that, if you ever need a politician's help. Senator Percy, finally realizing he had to say something, told me to contact Congressman Robert Michel of Peoria, Illinois. He said Michel was a friend of Nixon's and that he should be able to help me. Another point to remember, a politician will always pass the buck, if he or she can. And Senator Percy did.

However, this gave me another angle. I then telephoned Congressman Michel's office and demanded to talk to the congressman. I told them Senator Percy asked that I call. Well, there was no way the secretary was going to let me talk to the congressman. So, I had to explain what I wanted. She said that she would give the message to the congressman. She thought she could brush me off, however, she didn't know who she was dealing with!

I called again every day for a week. When you want something, you can't give up. Bug the heck out of them and they will usually give in. Just ask any eight-year-old. Parents always do for their kids, and husbands always do for their wives. So, why would a politician be any different? Finally, they gave in.

Congressman's Michel's secretary told me that the congressman was in, that she would talk to him, and call me right back. In about 30 minutes, she called me. She indicated that the congressman had talked to Nixon's office in San Clemente, California and that they were open to the idea. She said that I should write a detailed letter to Nixon's Chief of Staff Col. John Brennan and she gave me a special address. She didn't make any promises, but the congressman had opened the door for me. The rest was up to me.

I then wrote the letter of my life. I poured it on so strong; it looked like I worshiped the ground that Nixon walked on. (Some people thought I already did.) I think I even exaggerated a little in the letter, imagine that? I mailed it that day, because we were scheduled to leave for California in about a week.

Five days later, I was at my parents' home by myself, when the phone rang. You know who it was? It was Col. Brennan himself. He said that he had gotten my letter and that the former president would see me on August 1, 1978 at 10 A.M. He then gave me their private office number to call to confirm the time when I arrived in California.

Wow! I was in! You can't imagine how excited I was. There I was, an 18-year-old kid, about to graduate from high school, and about to meet a former president of the United States in his private home. A former president who was in isolation, who wasn't seeing anyone, who wasn't giving TV interviews at the time, was going to see me.

When I told my family and friends, most people didn't believe me. They actually thought I was making this up. In fact, when I told one of my relatives, they said, "How do you know that was Nixon's Office? That was probably a prank call!"

In fact, they even got me to question it. Could it really be a friend playing a joke on me? After all, several people knew that I was trying to get the appointment. Should I call the number they had given me to see if it was legitimate? If I called and it was, I would feel like a fool.

So, what I did was call the phone company information. First, I asked for the number for Richard Nixon. After they stopped laughing, they said that the number was unlisted. I then said, "I have a number, could you verify if it is Richard Nixon's number?" The operator referred me to a supervisor.

"I'm sorry, we can't do that, Mr. Wayman," she said. "The security on presidential numbers is as tight as Fort Knox. We don't even have the number." However, she did tell me that the number I had was indeed a San Clemente, California number.

That was good enough for me. I was convinced. I was going to meet my hero.

When my friend and I arrived in San Clemente, we wanted to find a hotel close to the Nixon estate. We had no idea where Nixon lived. We guessed we would have found it one way or the other. We stopped at one hotel, checked the price for a room, it was too high, so we moved on. Finally, our third stop was a hotel within our budget. After checking in, I asked the hotel clerk where Mr. Nixon lived. "His estate is just right across the road there. You can walk!" You can call that a coincidence, but I call it fate.

The next day we called the Nixon number, the number with security as tight as Fort Knox and they moved us to 10:30 A.M. That was cool; it didn't make any difference to us.

That morning when we arrived, I was excited. This was the moment that I had been waiting for. After checking in with the guard at the gate, we drove into the estate. We parked next to his home. His office was in a separate building next to the residence, which was called "La Casa Pacifica." It was the most beautiful estate I had ever seen.

We walked into the office to find another guard. It was a U.S. Marshall. He motioned us to the secretary. (The secretary had a broken nose at the time, which I know is not at all relevant to the story, but I thought it was interesting. She had a big bandage tapped on her nose. I asked her what had happened to her nose. She replied that she "broke it." Well, I already knew that, I guess, but I had to ask anyway.) Nevertheless, she was very nice and asked us to have a seat. "The president will be with you shortly," she said. Boy, I liked the sound of that. In fact, I'll say it again; "The president will be with you shortly."

A few minutes later, another couple walked into the office. I found out later that the gentleman was a member of the British Parliament. The lady was his wife.

We got called to go in first. As I walked in, my heart almost stopped; there he was, Richard Nixon, the 37th President of the United States of America. He walked toward me, shook my hand and I said, "It's great to meet you, Mr. President!"

For some strange reason, the man made me feel comfortable right away. A great calmness swept all over me. I just sat there and began talking to him, as if I had known him for years. In fact, he did the same to me. I think we hit it off, because we talked for nearly an hour while a member of the British Parliament was waiting in the room next door. Boy, did I feel important.

I asked him a lot of questions about his activities. He gave me a lot of advice. I asked him about China, about the Vietnam War, about the draft. He asked me about Illinois politics and about my future. One piece of advice he gave me was, "Don't be afraid to take chances. Those who take chances and lose are far better off than those who don't take chances at all."

At another point, he told us to "remember Lot's wife (from the Bible). Learn from your mistakes and don't look back." Oh, what good advice.

He also stated that he knew what I went through to get the appointment to see him. He said that he got hundreds of requests each week and that he appreciated my eagerness and consistency. "You were determined," he said, "and I like that."

I told him that I had gone to visit his boyhood home in Yorba Linda, California the previous day but was disappointed because I wasn't allowed to go inside. He apologized and said that an innkeeper lived there and it wasn't open for tours. (Footnote: Today it is. It's the home of the Nixon Library and birthplace. Mr. and Mrs. Nixon are also buried there.) He then said, "Maybe I can make it up to you. Would you like a tour of our estate here?" Of course, you know what the answer was.

He then called in one of his aides and asked him to take us on a tour. Before we left, he gave me a book he wrote and a presidential pen used for signing bills. He also signed several autographs for me.

While I was standing there waiting for the aide to come in, Mr. Nixon asked his secretary if the member of Parliament was there and waiting. She said he was. Nixon asked her how long he had waited. "For nearly an hour, Mr. President," she replied. His response was, "Oh, no!" Even a former president hates to have people wait. How come our medical doctors care less? Our doctors should take some lessons from this former president.

At that time, Mr. Nixon's dog ran into the office, jumped on me and started licking me in the face. "He likes you!" Nixon said. He went on to apologize for the dog. I told him that I loved dogs and no apology was needed.

As we departed, I told Nixon that I hoped to see him again some day. His response to me was, "Well, if I'm ever in Southern Illinois, I'll look you up." With that, we shook hands again, and I left the office.

His aide then escorted us outside to the "Richard Nixon Golf Cart," where we would tour the estate. Apparently, Nixon used it to drive himself back and forth from the main house to the office. The aide drove us all around and showed us the pool, the living room and the main entrance. You name it, we saw it.

At one point, we were driving and a guard up ahead blew a whistle and made a hand motion. Our driver immediately stopped and turned around. I asked what was going on. He said that Pat Nixon was working in the flower garden up ahead and would prefer not to greet visitors while she was dressed with her jeans and a sweatshirt. I quickly turned and looked. I did catch a glimpse of her, bent down, working in the flower garden.

With that, we left the estate. We had many pictures and a great memory. The man went the extra mile to treat us like we were important. I will never forget that day in August of 1978.

My story made the national news. A story was out on the Associated Press wire service about how a "tricky teen" got an appointment with a former president. I would like to see the look on the face of the editor of my home town newspaper, The Benton Evening News, when he saw the story come off of the AP Wire. I had just quit my paper routes with them a few months earlier. I used my paper money to go to California. The story made the front page of our newspaper.

The story was also on national radio and I had interviews on several television stations. WLS-TV out of Chicago even flew me to Chicago from Benton to appear on their local morning talk show, "AM Chicago." I really enjoyed the attention and telling them my Nixon story and how well Nixon treated us!

HOW I MET JOHNNY CARSON

It was in 1978, the same year I met Nixon.

It was another time when my "Benton Connections" paid off. When my friend Kent Alsobrooks and I were planning to see President Nixon in August of 1978, we were planning on spending about two weeks in the Los Angles area. We also knew that Lynn Bolin, a former Benton resident whose mother still lived in Benton, was the vice president of NBC Day Time Programming. We met her mother and asked that she contact her daughter to set up an appointment for us to meet her. She did.

Lynn's office was on the grounds of the 20th Century Fox studios in California. We arrived at the famous Fox gate you always see in movies and the guard had our names listed on the board and let us drive in. We parked the car and found her office.

During our short visit she asked if we wanted to see some shows while we were in LA. We asked to see "Welcome Back Kotter" and "The Tonight Show." She made some calls for us. "Welcome Back" was no problem, but the "Tonight Show" was hot and all the VIP tickets were gone. She could tell that we were disappointed. So she went the second mile and said, "I'll tell you what I will do. I will have my secretary meet you from inside and let you in at the door before the ticket holders come in."

After we left Lynn's office, she bought us dinner in the Fox Restaurant where all the stars ate. However, before we ate, she told us we could walk around the studio. We did just that. We saw them film "Love Boat," a pilot show Lynn was producing called "WEB," and the legendary TV Show "MASH."

When we were walking into the studio that was marked "Love Boat," there was a sign on the door with the words, "Do Not Enter when Light is On." We did not see the sign and we walked in on the action. The director yelled, "Cut!" We were cussed out and asked who we were and what we were doing there. We said we were guests of Lynn Bolin and we were touring the studio. The director even called her office to confirm and said that we could stay for 5 minutes! The scene was exciting because it was a love scene in a ship cabin with none other than celebrities Sid Ceaser and Ruth Buzbee.

Our "Tonight Show" visit was the most exciting. That night when we went to the "Tonight Show," we went past the long line of people trying to get in. We went past the VIP booth, straight to the door. At our scheduled time, Lynn Bolin's secretary was waiting for us inside. We walked in. We were the first in the studio. She had us sit anywhere we wanted and we waited in an empty studio. About 10 minutes later the studio audience came in.

On the show, the guests listed on the sign outside included Erma Bombeck, Johnny Mathis and some unknown comic. However, during the show Johnny was interrupted by the producer. Johnny said, "We have a surprise guest! He needs no introduction."

Dean Martin walked onto the stage and the audience went wild. Dean had indicated that he was driving by Burbank and remembered that it was the time that the show was usually filmed. He said he had not seen his good friend Johnny Carson lately and called to see if he could come by and say hi. It was unrehearsed, spontaneous and very funny. The only joke I can remember is that Dean had a drink in his hand and Dean said, "Johnny, this is the first drink I had today (pause), with my left hand!"

My visit to the Tonight Show was a great experience. We will miss you, Johnny!

MY SPANISH CLASS
"HOW'S NORMAN?"

When I was in high school I wanted to learn Spanish. I took a semester of "Introduction to Spanish" because I knew that foreign language was required in college with my major. I wanted to get a head start. I joined the Spanish Club in high school and even went with them on a trip to Spain. (Just a piece of advice, when people say you can learn a foreign language by going to a foreign country, they are lying. Take if from me, you can't!)

In Spain, I was lost. All I could say was "Hello, how are you?" and "I don't speak Spanish." To this day, I can remember how to say it, but I can't spell it. (That's why I'm writing this in English and not Spanish.)

When I went to college, I had to take two semesters of Spanish. I had a hard time. I spent a lot of effort with the class, but couldn't learn the language. In class, I was the laughing stock. Our teacher, a young lady from Mexico, could never remember my name. She always called me Norman by mistake. (I guess Gordon does sound like Norman, especially in Spanish.) I would always correct her, and she would say, "I'm sorry, Gordon" and five seconds later, she would call me "Norman" again. The class would always die laughing. I finally got to a point that I gave up and stopped correcting her. Every time she called my name out, the class would laugh. However, she could never figure out why the class thought my name was so funny.

When we first started the class, the teacher knew right off that I would have problems. Right before the deadline for dropping classes, she called me into her office and said, "Norman, there are people who can learn foreign language and there are people who can't. Unfortunately, you are one of those who can't!" Well, at least she was honest.

Since I couldn't drop the class because it was required, I took it Pass/Fail. We were allowed to take only two classes in four years Pass/Fail, so I figured Spanish should be it. All I had to do was make a "D" or better and my records would record "P." No one would know that I had a hard time.

On the last day of class, our Spanish teacher put all the grades up on the board. She said one person did not make it. My heart almost stopped. Did I go through a semester of hell for nothing? Then she said another student made a "D." If it weren't for the extra credit lab work, this student too would have failed. I felt better, because I was that student. Of all my grades in college, I was most proud of that "D," or "P," I received in Spanish!

CHAPTER 5

THINK OF STUPID THINGS YOU DID

When you're doing your business you can also think about stupid things you did at one time or another in your life. These could be things you did in your youth, in your middle age, or just today. Here are some examples.

THE CHINESE RESTAURANT
"PROUD TO LIVE IN THE USA!"

Several years ago, when I was in college (well, it wasn't that long ago, because I have been 29 for several years now), I had some friends who would always try to get me to do things I didn't want to do. You know the type. People who tell you, "No, that roller coaster doesn't go down very deep at all," and you get on it and it's the biggest one in the world! That type.

One evening we were going to go out to dinner. My friends wanted to go to a Chinese restaurant, but they knew that I hated Chinese food. My philosophy is, "What country do we live in, anyway?" I'm an American and plan to eat American food, like pizza and French fries! Well, that evening one of my friends said let's have a drink before we go out for dinner. I really didn't want anything, because I am not a very big drinker. But they insisted on giving me some vodka and tonic. I had never had that drink before. And I found out later that they put about 4/5s vodka in the drink. They also kept hurrying me up to drink it as quick as I could. Well, you can guess what happened. I got drunk very quickly.

As soon as they realized that I was pretty wasted, we got in the car and headed to the Chinese restaurant. When we got there, I was making a scene with my patriotic routine. I didn't know what to order. They said that I could order some chicken and rice and ask them to cook it "American style." I am told, because I was so drunk that I did not really remember it, that I told the waiter: "If you have to serve me Chinese food, then put an American flag in it and sing the Star-Spangled Banner to me when you serve it!"

EMBARRASSING MOMENTS
"IF THEY COULD SEE ME NOW?"

We all have moments that we look back on and say, "I can't believe that happened." Well, I have my share of embarrassing moments.

One day I was at my desk in my office. At this time I was an assistant manager. An employee had just given me a toy car from a kid's meal at a local fast food restaurant. I was alone in my office, playing with the car, moving it up and down on my desk making a car-like noise, when the deputy director walked into my office. He looked at me and laughed, "Oh, you're real busy, huh Gordon." Well, to my advantage he had a sense of humor. We both laughed, but my face turned as red as a tomato.

On another occasion, I was in my office when some sort of national incident occurred. I think it may have been the explosion of the space shuttle, or something like that. One of the employees had a little TV in her car, so I asked her to bring it into my office, and during our break we would watch the news. I told my boss about the TV and she was going to come down to watch it too. The employee came into my office with the small TV. I was sitting in my chair behind my desk. She put the TV on the desk, and got on her knees to plug in the TV. The plug-in was located underneath my desk. I moved my chair back a little, so she could crawl under the entrance to my desk. Do you have the picture? Guess what happened? At that time, my boss walked into my office.

There I was, sitting in a chair at my desk, and a second later, a girl came up from the floor from under my desk. Again, my face turned red, and I said, "This is not as it seems!"

Fast Food Restaurants
"I'll Take a Hot Fudge Sunday Instead!"

Don't you just love fast food restaurants? They all try their best to do something to get you in the door. They spend fortunes on advertising, promotions, and toys for the kids, etc. You wonder why every kid in America loves these places? Who wouldn't? They give you stuff free with your meal. We all want something "free." And they have our kids wanting these wonderful toys with their hamburgers. In fact, this one kid I know ate at fast food places for so long he expected a toy with every meal. The kid wouldn't eat until he got a toy. This got to be expensive for the parents.

A few years ago, one of the fast food restaurants had the slogan, "Sometimes you have to break the rules." No one really knew what it meant, but it did sound good. Break the rules, eat fast food. Whatever?

One day I was at the "Break the Rules" fast food place, when I ordered their special that included a free plastic cup with a soft drink. The cup had a picture of a popular movie. (This toy was for adults too.) I told them I wanted it with a milk shake. The employee said, "I'm sorry, we can't do that." My immediate response was, "But, you say in your commercial that sometimes you have to break the rules!" The manager overheard the conversation. He said, "Your right! Give him the shake!"

On another occasion, I was eating at another fast food restaurant, when I noticed that the amount of toppings in the salad seemed really skimpy. In fact, I had ordered the same salad in the same fast food joint several times in the past, and I had never received so little cheese and carrots. After I had finished the salad, one of their employees was walking around asking people if everything was ok. Don't you just love it when they do that? They really don't want you to give them the truth, because as Jack Nicholson would say, "They can't handle the truth!"

This time I was going to speak up. The lady asked, "How was your meal?" My response was, "Terrible. In fact," I said, "I have ordered this salad several times in the past and I was really disappointed. Are you trying to save money and cut down on the toppings?" I asked. "No sir. I'm very sorry," she said. "Would you like another salad?" What was a question like that? I already ate. I didn't want another salad, I thought. "No," I said, "but I'll take a hot fudge sunday with nuts instead!"

Sometime it pays to think fast!

MIXING WORDS
"I MEANT TO SAY . . ."

I'm the worst person there is for pronouncing words. I always either mispronounce the word, or use the wrong word in a sentence. I am usually close, so people know what I am talking about, but often I'm really far off.

Let me give you some examples. In 1984, I took the big step and went from renting an apartment to purchasing a condo unit. I was really excited and proud of my new condo. It was my first piece of real estate. However, every time I told people about it, I would use a word that is similar but has a totally different meaning. I would say, "I just love my new condo*m!* It's so big. It's much bigger than I'm used to. Would you like to come over and see it?"

On another occasion, I was in Miami with a friend. We were standing in line at a fancy restaurant for dinner waiting for a table. We were talking to one of the employees. The employee, realizing that we sounded different, asked us where we were from. My response was, "Oh, we are not from around here. We are just terrorists!" Of course I meant to say "tourists." Needless to say, we did get a table right away in that Miami restaurant and we were treated very special that night!

THE SUBMARINE EXPERIENCE
"AVOID AT ALL COST!"

My wife and I enjoy taking cruises. During one of our cruises to the Caribbean, we were reading in a travel book, that we were not to miss the Atlantis Submarine ride on one of the islands. In fact, our travel agent went as far as to say, "You haven't experience the Caribbean until you go on the submarine." In fact, in one book, it stated that many felt the submarine was the "highlight of the trip."

So, giving into peer pressure, we decided to go on the submarine excursion. A boat would pick us up at a certain location, and then take us out in the middle of the ocean, where the submarine would meet us. Then we would board the submarine to go to the depths of the ocean for an hour. Sounds fun? And at the end of the trip we would get a certificate to certify us as an Official Atlantis Submariner! Wow! We couldn't wait.

When we boarded the boat to go to the submarine, the ocean was rough. In fact, the boat rocked back and forth so much, my wife and I got very sick. My wife had read previously in a women's magazine that if you ate crackers it would help settle your stomach. Well, take it from us, it doesn't work, especially for seasickness. My wife and I both vomited the crackers right up in a bag on the boat.

It took us a good 45 minutes to make it to the submarine. By that time, we were sicker than a dog. In fact,

I wanted to go back, right then! However, the guide told me we had to wait or go in the submarine. They said that the water was much calmer underneath then in the boat, so we elected to go in the submarine.

This submarine was so small we couldn't believe it. In fact, they should have been arrested to even call it a submarine. It was only about 10 feet wide. It fit about 40 people sitting on top of each other facing one way. Twenty people each way would sit with their backs touching, facing the opposite direction. Talk about claustrophobia? We really had it.

We had to sit there all as tight as sardines for one hour as the submarine got lower and lower beneath the sea. The sights were nice. We could see beautiful fish and ship wreckage, however, it was HELL! We couldn't wait until it got back up to the boat. However, the boat ride home was also HELL. As soon as we got back, we got our certificate, because we really earned it, and headed back to our cabin in the big cruise ship. We went straight to bed.

If you ever go on a cruise, don't listen to the travel agent about the submarine. Take it from me; avoid it at all cost!

RETURN TO SENDER
"WHY DON'T WE ALL TRY THIS?"

Don't you just hate it when you send a letter, put one stamp on it, and it comes back to you "Return to Sender - Insufficient Postage?" Doesn't it cost the post office more to send it back asking for one more stamp? Once I sent a letter and forgot to put any postage on it, and it came back. This got my wife thinking and she came up with this idea: Why don't we put the address we really want the letter to go to in the sender spot, and our address as the addressee? When we reverse it, then it would go postage free, wouldn't it?

That would really show them.

CHAPTER 6

MY LETTERS

When I have bad experiences either from a hotel visit or dealing with bad businesses, I always feel better when I sit down and write a letter. Sometimes I get free stuff as a result, but most the time I get nothing. However, I really feel better. When you feel good, it is much easier to relax so you can do your business in that special room. Enjoy.

THE CAR RENTAL
"I HAVE A RESERVATION!"

What is it with the car rental companies in America? How do they define reservation? For the average person, when a reservation is made, it means something is "held" for you. You "reserve" something so you will have the peace of mind that when you are ready to pick it up, it will be there waiting for you. However, with car rental companies "reservation" has a different meaning. It means, "We will type it in the computer and if we didn't give your car away to someone else, you may get a car."

When I attended a business conference in Charlotte, North Carolina, I had an interesting experience with a car rental company. My experience resulted in this letter:

• • • • • • •

Dear Sir or Madam:

I recently stayed at the Adam's Mark Hotel in Charlotte, North Carolina. Your company has a branch office located at the hotel where cars can be rented directly from the hotel.

On Friday, November 6, 1998 I talked to your employee and reserved a car for Saturday, November 7, 1998. I told your employee my room number and that I would pick the car up "around noon." She typed the information into the computer and told me that I was all set and that she "would be there."

I got out of my meeting at noon and went to the counter. I saw that she was with another customer, so I figured that I had time to change clothes. I went up to my room and changed clothes. I came down at exactly 12:10 and she was gone! I asked the hotel clerk where she was, and they said that she always leaves at noon on Saturday.

I called your airport branch and told them about my situation. They said that they could not help me unless I wanted to come out there. I asked if they could bring me a car. They said no, that they were short handed. There I was, stuck in Charlotte, with no car. I tried to find another car rental company but had no luck.

What kind of business are you running? I deal with rental car agencies allot and never seen such bad practice. If she was going to leave at noon, why didn't she tell me when I made the reservation? She could have said, "Make sure you're here by noon, because I will leave at noon, sharp!" Then, I would have made sure I was there. She had my room number, why didn't she call me before she left? I was in my room on my way down.

I just thought you would want to know how your employees are hurting your business. I will think twice before I use your company again.

Sincerely,
Gordon D. Wayman

· · · · · · ·

My letter was sent to the president and CEO of the car rental company in question. A few days after I mailed my letter, I received a response from the president of the company. He indicated that he had received my letter and was very concerned about the situation that I had outlined. He indicated that he would turn my case over for investigation and that their company would get back with me in the next ten days.

With that letter, I was already impressed with the company. At least they were concerned about my situation. In about ten days, I received what I believe was the best response I had ever received from any company. The person who wrote this letter received my vote of confidence. This is what the letter said:

· · · · · · ·

Dear Mr. Wayman:

Thank you for taking the time to write to us. We appreciate customers who let us know when things aren't right. Without question, we failed to deliver the level of service you expect and deserve and for that I sincerely apologize.

You are absolutely correct. You should have been told at the time of your reservation that our Char-

lotte location has a closing time of noon. We were extremely embarrassed after reading your letter. The frustration and inconvenience we caused you is no more acceptable to us than it was to you. Please accept my sincere and unreserved apology for the entire incident.

I am sorry that the airport location was not able to solve the problems you encountered. The manager of our Charlotte locations has been notified of your comments and assures us that corrective measurers have been taken to ensure that this situation is never repeated.

As concrete form of apology, I have enclosed three free day certificates. Your goodwill is important to us and we wish to make amends for your unhappy experience.

I hope you are persuaded to think a little less harshly of us. We value you as a customer and we are eager to restore your confidence. Please give us another opportunity to serve you. In turn we will do our best to make your rental pleasant and trouble free.

· · · · · · ·

Now that's a letter! Those of you who are in customer service can learn a great deal from this letter. First, the company admitted that I was treated poorly. The letter was not a form letter because he specifically addressed my situation. Second, he assured me that he was taking action with his staff to stop this from happening to other customers in the future. Third, he gave me something free, three free car rentals, that was a "payment" for my bad experience. And finally, he pleaded for me to think "less harshly" of his company.

The letter worked. To this day I use that company.

MY LONDON HOTEL EXPERIENCE
"OH, WHAT COMFORT!"

In 1996, my wife and I went to London, England to celebrate our second wedding anniversary (this was my third trip to London). While there, we stayed at a hotel that had a motto of being extra friendly and comfortable. Our experience there resulted in me writing the following letter to the Hotel Corporate Office.

• • • • • • •

Dear Sir:

I would like to write about our recent experience with your hotel, in Kenningston, London, England, United Kingdom. Our stay was neither "Comfortable" nor "Friendly."

My wife and I arrived at your hotel exhausted due to our 9-hour flight from the United States. We arrived at 1 P.M. on Thursday, May 23rd, 1996. I approached the front desk with only one customer ahead of me. That customer checked in, and now it was my turn. Right before the clerk was about to check us in, the manager came to the counter. She informed us that check-in time was 2 P.M. and the rooms were not ready yet. Apparently, the customer ahead of us got the last clean room. So, we waited.

As we waited, 15 minutes passed by, another customer arrived and they were told that check-in time was 2 P.M. That customer waited; 30 minutes went by, another customer arrived; 45 minutes, another customer, and still no rooms. The manager waited until exactly 2 P.M. When the second hand on the clock arrived exactly on the 12, she announced "Check-In Time!"

I have a hard time believing that all of the rooms were ready exactly at 2 P.M. and no rooms were ready at 1:15, or 1:45, or 1:55 P.M.! The manager stood at the counter during this hour doing nothing while her customers were miserable. She seemed to really enjoy displaying her authority over the situation.

After we checked into our room, the drama continues! Our travel agency had informed us that the room would be two double beds. Instead it had one full size bed. We called the front desk. The manager said no, that the reservation was for one bed. She was right, we were wrong.

Our stay was for 8 nights. On the third day, I had just finished taking a shower when the manager knocked at our door. I answered the door with a towel around my body. She asked if I had just taken a shower. I answered, "Yes." She said that the water from our room was leaking downstairs, and we had to move to another room. We had to pack up everything after 3 days and move. It took us an hour to do. I asked the manger if we would get something for our trouble, a discount, a complimentary dinner, or something. She said, "NO!"

I cannot believe how rude she was. Our drama continues. When we got to the new room I could tell right away that the room's air conditioner did not work as well as the previous room. I did not say anything because it was cool outside. However, on our 6th day there our room was very hot. We had the air conditioner on high for 24 hours and it did not cool the room. We called the front desk. They sent their maintenance man. I told him that I believed there was something wrong with the air conditioner. He told me, "Oh, it's just extremely hot today. I'll be glad to open a window for you!" He then got up on a chair, and took nails out of the window (it had been nailed shut). After he finished, he said, "Is there anything else I can do?" I shook my head in amazement. He did not even check the air conditioner; he just opened a window!

We were very hot for our last two days in the hotel. We checked out on May 31st knowing that we would probably never stay in your hotel again!

I am a manager and deal with the public every day. I would never treat customers the way your people do. I could not believe it. We travel a lot and stay in hotels all over the world. I hope you improve your service in the future. If you do not, I believe your company will really suffer. When customers are unhappy with their service they tell others. We have told several of my employees and several of our friends. We will continue to do so. You may spend millions of dollars in television advertising, however, that advertising is all in vain when your service is terrible.

Thank you for taking the time to read this letter.

Sincerely,

Gordon Wayman

. . . .

The above letter is true and speaks for itself. That's my story and I'm sticking to it! The Hotel Office never responded to my letter.

MY ST. PAUL HOTEL EXPERIENCE
"EXCEEDING YOUR EXPECTATION"

I had another bad experience at a hotel when I attended a work conference for the AAMVA (American Association of Motor Vehicle Administrators). Yes, I know that's a mouth full! That's why we call it AAMVA.

At this hotel, they even try to "exceed your expectations," and they use that phase all over the hotel. Don't you just hate it when businesses have slogans that brag about customer service? And when they fail, they just look at you and smile, "Well, I'm sorry Mr. Wayman."

Once, I was in a retail store where they had a big sign hanging over the cash registers with these words, "Our Guarantee to You: When there are 3 or more people in line we will open another register. Our customers come first!" In the line I was in, there were 6 people in line. In fact, every register had more than 3 people in line. I said something to one of the employees. Their response was, "Oh, we're sorry, we are just extra busy today!" Well, then what is the purpose of the guarantee! I can't figure out some businesses. Nevertheless, this letter is another example of such a business.

· · · · · · ·

Dear Sir:

I wanted to write you directly to inform you about my recent experience at your hotel.

As a manager myself for a large agency, I am sure that you are sincere about trying to improve service. You stated in your brochure that your company is "determined not only to meet expectations, but to exceed them." Well, your hotel in St. Paul, did not meet my expectations at all. Here's why:

1. The Soap Incident

Your hotel housekeeper must be the type who takes giving out soap as if it was coming from her personal account. When I checked in there were two tiny bars of soap in my room: one for your face and the other for the shower. This was fine. However, the next day the soap was almost gone, but she did not replace the bars. It is common practice in other hotels to always place an extra bar soap in a box in the bathroom.

I called your hotline and requested more soap. I waited but received no soap. I had to hurry to a meeting, so I had to leave. Three hours later, when I returned to my hotel room, I was expecting the soap to be there, but it wasn't! I called your hotline again, they said there was a mix-up and they would get it to me right away. They did, within 15 minutes, which was fine but they only gave me one extra bar.

After the one soap incident, you would think that the housekeeper would have been told to make sure you put extra soap in the rooms, customers are complaining. The next day, the same thing happened. No new soap. The third day, I was down to the very last piece (the bars are also too small). I thought for sure she would fill the soap the third day. NO, she did not!

I called your hotline again. This time I asked what was going on, was the hotel trying to conserve soap or what? They said no and this time brought me up three bars, which was more than enough to hold me over until I checked out.

2.   The Hot Room

The second day I realized that something was wrong with the air conditioner. The setting was as high as it would go, 55 degrees, and it wasn't close to 55 degrees. It was about 80. The air was running, but it was not cool enough. I kept it on full blast for two days and it did not cool the room like other hotels I have been in. So I called your hotline again. They said they would send someone to look at it.

I was gone when they came. They left a message on my voice mail saying that they had fixed it. They did not. I did not call back, because I knew the only answer that they would have given was to move me into another room. I did not have the time to do this. So, I gave up and slept uncomfortably for my entire five day stay.

3.   The Leak!

If you think that was not enough, there's more. When I got back to my room on the 4th day, there was water leaking big time in the hall under the air conditioner. I called your hotline for the fourth time. They said they would send someone. I was in the room for the next hour and no one came. I had to leave for another meeting. When I returned the leaking was gone, but there was no note or message on my voice mail. I assume they fixed it, or it just went away on its own.

In conclusion, as a CEO, you should know what is going on in your organization. That is why I have chosen to contact you directly. Thank you for taking the time to read this letter.

Sincerely,

Gordon Wayman

• • • • • • •

I don't know what it is about the hotels I go to, but it seems to me that they all have it out for me. You will read of several of my hotel experiences in this book.

MY OMAHA HOTEL EXPERIENCE
"THE 5 A.M. WAKE-UP ALARM!"

What is it about me and hotels? Everywhere I go, I always have something to report about the hotel. Sometimes I wonder if there is a hotel conspiracy. When Gordon Wayman checks in, give him Hell!

In Omaha, Nebraska, I was awaken by an alarm clock at 5 A.M. (two and a half hours before my scheduled wake-up call). And, to top it off, it blasted for almost one hour before the hotel would turn it off!

Here's the letter I wrote to the president and CEO.

• • • • • • •

Dear Sir:

I recently stayed at your hotel in Omaha, Nebraska. I attended a pre-planning meeting for the conference of the AAMVA that was held in the same hotel July 9–13, 1999.

As Chairman for one of the Committees of AAMVA, I have had the opportunity to travel to many hotels. The experience I had at your hotel has to be at the bottom of the list. I wanted to write you personally about my experience, because as president and CEO, you need to know what is going on in your hotels.

I checked in on Friday, January 22, 1999 for our pre-planning meeting. After a long day and flight, I was looking forward to the "Sweat Dreams" you proudly proclaim in your brochure. I went to bed around 11:30 P.M. and asked for a wake-up call at 7:30 A.M.

My wake-up call did not come at 7:30 A.M., but instead, I was awaken at 5 A.M. by the alarm clock in the room next to me. After hearing the alarm clock blasting for 15 minutes, I called your "CARE line" and explained the situation. The operator said that they would check into it. I went back to bed, put some pillows over my head, and waited. I waited another 15 minutes. By now, the alarm clock had been blasting for 30 minutes!

I called the front desk again. This time I was angry. I told the operator that the alarm was driving me crazy and asked if something could be done. He explained that he had called it in the first time and would call it in again. At no time did he apologize or appear sympathized with my situation. Instead, he said in an angry voice that he would call it in again. I went back to bed waiting, playing again the wait game. Five minutes more went by, five minutes more. As I waited, I became angrier.

I called again at 5:50 A.M. This ordeal has lasted 50 minutes! On the third telephone call, the operator started to argue with me. He said the lady went to the room, and heard no alarm clock. I requested that she come directly to my room. A few minutes later, I could hear her walkie-talkie in the hall, with the voice "He called again!"

I went to my door, and invited the lady in to listen. She immediately heard the noise and said, "Oh it's the room on the other side!" She had been going to room 930 and all along it was room 926! At that point, I lost it, "Does it take a rocket scientist to figure out that the room next to you could mean on either side?" In addition, if you went to one room and the alarm clock was not blasting, would you not automatically check the room on the other side? She finally went into room 926, which was empty, and turned the alarm clock off. The time was 5:53 A.M. The alarm clock had blasted for 53 minutes!

The next day, as part of the Conference Planning Committee, your Customer Service Manager gave us a tour of the hotel. During the tour she explained that Doubletree was big on customer service and that we could call the CARE number 24 hours a day and they would immediately respond to the needs of the guests. I raised my hand and said, "Well, they certainty did not at 5 A.M. this morning?" I went on to tell her my story. She attempted to defend her staff and said that they ended up going to the wrong room. She quickly got off the subject and finished her tour. It was obvious she did not want to talk about it.

Here are my complaints:

The problem should have been taken care of in 10 to 15 minutes, not 53 minutes!

The operator should have been polite, said he was "sorry" and appear sympathetic.

Once it was obvious that the room was not 930, the person should have checked 926, or asked me what room it was. I could have gone down the hall and checked the room number, or informed them the direction of the room.

When the lady finally came to my room at 5:53 A.M., she could have apologized or appeared sympathetic to my situation. She did not. She appeared frustrated.

When I explained my situation the day after during the hotel tour, your employee should have not found excuses, but apologized. In addition, she should have gotten me aside privately after the tour and apologized again.

Sir, your hotel staff in Omaha gave me the worst experience I have had with any hotel. One of the questions in your "Because We Care" survey was "Will you return?" Unfortunately, I have to because of the conference in July. If it were not for that, I would never again return.

And to top all of this off, I returned back to my room at 4:30 P.M. the next day to get some rest before dinner since I got up so early on Saturday morning. What did I find? My room had not been cleaned yet. I had to wait in the hall another 30 minutes before my room was cleaned! I have never stayed at a hotel where return guests have their room cleaned between 4:30 and 5 P.M. With *this, I only could rest a few minutes before dinner.*

As president and CEO, I thought you would want to know about my experience.

Sincerely,

Gordon Wayman

• • • • • • •

This is another letter that I received no response from. No apology, no form letter, nothing.

There is a funny antidote to the story, however. The next day after the incident, I was sitting in the restaurant. The table next to me was an older lady, at least 80. I overheard her conversation. "You won't believe what happened to me last night," she told her friend. "At 5 A.M., the hotel manager pounded on my door insisting that I turn off my alarm clock!"

A Special Invitation
"Women Like Me"

Don't you just love all the junk mail we get? If it weren't for junk mail, my mailbox would be empty on most days. One day I received a unique letter addressed to "Gordon Wayman" from a woman's magazine with a special invitation to subscribe to the magazine. I had never heard of the magazine, but when I read the letter, I learned that the magazine was a Christian Magazine for women. The letter was **not** addressed to "Mrs. Gordon Wayman," but to "Gordon." (I wasn't married at the time, anyway.) For some reason, the magazine had me down as a woman.

This was the first time that I had been mistaken for a woman, so I thought I would have some fun by writing a letter. I wrote to the Publisher of the magazine the following:

· · · · · · ·

Dear Madam:

Thank you for your letter inviting me to take advantage of your generous special introductory offer to your fine magazine, "The Christian Magazine for Women."

However, I regret to inform you that I am not the kind of Christian woman you referred to in your letter. I have no desire to be "the kind of wife, mother, and woman" you refer to.

In addition, I have no desire "to be recognized as a woman who has self-worth, talents, and ideas to contribute to our world."

You see, I am not the type of woman who would subscribe to your fine magazine. I'm sorry that you started publishing your magazine for "women like me."

I have to decline your fine offer, because, you see, I am a man.

Sincerely,

Gordon Wayman

· · · · · · ·

Unfortunately, the editor did not respond to my letter. However, I never received anything else from that magazine.

CHAPTER 7

LAUGH YOURSELF TO SLEEP

Sometimes, we have to do our business at night before we go to bed, before we fall asleep. Why not fall asleep with a smile on your face? What follows are more stories intended for the evening session in that small room.

SWEAT DREAMS
"WHAT A NIGHT!"

I have always had a big imagination. When I was a child, I would play mind games, coming up with wild stories and imaginative experiences. During the last few years, I have taken notes about some of my wild dreams that I have had through the night. I would like to take you to some of the highpoints.

First, one of the weirdest dreams that I have had over the years could actually be an episode for "The Twilight Zone." I dreamed that there I was standing in a city. Everything was silent. I was walking down a street full of houses, but everything looked unlived in, perfect, like toy dollhouses. I went into one house. The house was full of furniture, but it did not look lived in. I went into the kitchen and opened the cabinets to find them empty. There was nothing in the refrigerator, nothing in the closets and nothing in the house but furniture.

I walked outside and yelled, "Anyone here!" and I could hear my echo bouncing off the empty houses down the street. Where was I? Where were all the people? It was like I was the only person on the planet.

I ran down the street into one house after the other, finding more of the same. Nothing. No people, no one. Each house had furniture, but they all looked unlived in.

Finally, I heard music. The music seemed far away. I ran towards it, down the street. It was the sound of a marching band. I ran and ran. Finally, I came to a parade. The people in the parade, however, were not normal. They were human, but they were staring straight ahead with no expressions on their faces, just marching, playing their music, like robots.

I went up to one and started talking to him, but he did not respond to me, he just looked straight ahead. Finally, I saw someone I recognized. It was my Aunt Dorothy! She too was looking straight ahead. I immediately woke up, very scared!

My aunt had been dead for over 20 years!

WORKING 9 TO 5
"JOKES ANYONE?"

Working for state government always makes you vulnerable for jokes. Some of the state employees play the part real well. For example, I know one guy who thinks his workday starts when he gets out of bed. If he works 9 to 5, that means he gets up at 9 A.M. and arrives back home by 5 P.M. Sounds good to me!

I was talking to the same guy one day and I asked him why he got his haircut in the middle of the day during working hours. His response was, "My hair grows on company time, so I'm going to get it cut on company time!"

An employee like that helps explain why the following joke was told. "Why does a state employee not look out of the window in the morning?" The answer, "So, he'll have something to do in the afternoon!"

My pastor, Bob Isringhausen, used to tell this joke: Three young boys were bragging about their fathers. One boy said that his dad was so fast he could shoot a bow and arrow, run and catch it before it reached its target. The other boy said that he could top that, his dad was so fast that he could shoot a gun and run and catch the bullet before it reached its target. Finally, the son of the state government employee said that he could beat both of their stories. "My dad works for the state. He's so fast, he gets off work at 5 and is home by 3!"

MOTOR VEHICLE STORIES
"SAY WHAT?"

I have worked for the agency in the state that issues drivers' licenses for over 20 years. Over the years, I have heard several funny incidents from various individuals. Some of them may be true, and some may not be.

First of all, I would like to say, I was a terrible driver in high school. When I was taking driver's education, I had several close calls. The other students were scared to death when I got behind the wheel. In fact, my instructor, Mr. Ken Hungate, believed I was the worst student he had. He asked me once, "Are you going to go out and practice driving tonight?" I responded, "Yes." My instructor then made this comment, "Before you go out, would you please give me a call, and I'll make sure I stay home."

My first story was told to me many years ago, before I even worked for the DMV. It is about a little old lady. It goes like this: One day, an examiner in a license facility somewhere in America, was giving a driving test to a lady around 80 years old. Part of the test consisted of the applicant performing various simple tasks in the vehicle. The lady was asked to turn on her left turn signal. She did. She was then asked to turn on her lights. She did. She was then asked to back up. She did. She was then asked to honk her horn. She did. Then the 80 year old lady made this remark, "What do you want me to do next, honey, fart?"

Another lady was stuck in a daily routine. Once, her office had mandatory overtime, where everyone had to work a specific Saturday unless they had a major emergency. Those with emergency situations were asked to go visit the manager. One employee came in and said she could not work on Saturday. When asked why, she responded, "Well, that's the day I get gas." She was not trying to be funny. She was totally serious. In her routine, the only day the gas station was opened was on Saturday.

It is also funny how we hear stories of how people get out of traffic violations. My late pastor and good friend Bob Isringhausen always told this story about his wife, Camille. The two of them were in the car when they got stopped by the police for going through a stoplight. The officer asked why he didn't stop at the stoplight. Camille, trying to help, bent over to address the officer through the window, and said, "But officer, we were going to fast to stop!" The officer stood there in amazement and said, "That's the best I've heard all day. Get out of here!"

DEALING WITH OTHER MANAGERS "THE STEP CHILD"

At my job, I am always the one that is picked on by other managers on our team. Imagine that? My office is on the first floor while the all the other mangers in my division as well as my boss reside on the second floor. I don't know what it is, but those who reside "above" you always seem "superior." I often think of myself as a stepchild or the Rodney Dangerfield of our division, I get no respect!

I am known for my funny story telling when we go to lunch as a group for special occasions. I am also known for mentioning things, nearly every time, about my home town of Benton, Illinois. One day I was called to my boss Terry Montalbano's office on my break. When I walked in all the other managers including my boss had Benton Ranger t-shirts on. John Kruger, one of the managers, had passed though my home town and picked them up at a store there. They just laughed and laughed. They thought it was so funny. (Note: "Rangers" is the mascot for our school sport teams.)

A few months later one of the managers, Tom Wekony who lived in the Chicago area, was going to go to a concert. The only t-shirt he had cleaned was the Benton one. So he actually wore his t-shirt to a concert in the city. When he went to the bathroom, someone saw him and started to eye him at the urinal. He thought, oh no, one of those types, when the person finally spoke and asked him about his t-shirt. The guy was actually from Benton originally. Now, Benton is a small town of 7,000 people nearly 400 miles from Chicago. What a small world!

A few months later, Tom and Terry were in Washington, D.C. for a conference. They were there the same time the boy scouts were having their convention. The two were walking in the Washington Mall by the Lincoln Memorial. They saw thousands of teenage boys running around making a lot of noise. Then they saw a small group of well-behaved boys sitting in a circle singing nice songs and some of them had bibles. Tom made the comment to Terry, "Those boys must be from Benton!" Terry laughed and didn't think much more about it. A few hours later they were on their way out when they saw a bus. Guess what was on the bus? A logo from Benton, Illinois. They actually freaked out. Benton people are everywhere! They are taking over the planet!

On one occasion we were going to lunch with all the managers. It happened to be around Memorial Day and about 20 minutes into the lunch I mentioned that the founder of Memorial Day, John A. Logan, actually lived in Benton. When I mentioned "Benton" everyone laughed. Apparently, there was a bet on how long it would be before I mentioned "Benton" during the lunch. My boss Terry won!

Once, I got several of the women mad at me during one of our luncheons. The men, however, would not stick up for me and just let me get beaten up. Somehow the topic of cooking out on the grill came up. One of the girls indicated that she was going to cook out on the grill. I told her that cooking out on the grill was a "man's job." "Women," I said, "have no business cooking on the grill." I got in real trouble with the women. If you are really honest, who does most of the grill cooking in America? I think it is known as a job for the man of the house, not the lady. No one would back me up, but I know that deep inside, they know that I am right!

MY AAMVA STORIES
"MY DAYS AS COMMITTEE CHAIR"

I have worked for the Secretary of State as Manager of the Safety and Financial Responsibility Section since 1984. For nearly four years I served as International Chair for the Financial Responsibility and Insurance (FRI) Committee for the American Association of Motor Vehicle Administrators (AAMVA).

It is not uncommon for people to get confused on what "Financial Responsibility" is. In the beginning of my chairmanship, the name of our committee was simply "Financial Responsibility" or FR for short. The word FR is a legal term used for individuals who drive vehicles. The law requires drivers to be "financially responsible" for damages they may cause in the event of a crash. The Motor Vehicle Departments will suspend drivers' licenses if people are not responsible.

When I first became Chairman of the FR Committee my first goal was to get more states involved in the committee. I had asked one specific state for a contact person. They finally gave me a name. When I contacted the individual he seemed confused when I started talking to him about insurance related issues. I later found out that he was an accountant and his boss had told him to be on the FR Committee to make AAMVA more "financially responsible." So after that I asked the association to change the name to add "Insurance" in the title. So we became the FRI Committee.

The name of our committee is also the name of my job title at work. I am Manager of the "Safety and Financial Responsibility Section" for the Secretary of State. Several years ago I received a letter from an individual who was confused with the meaning of our name as well. In the letter he was complaining about an individual who had a pet crocodile who lived in his apartment building. The owner would let the crocodile out of the cage in the apartment and it was not uncommon for the crocodile to get loose out the window and in the halls. The owner would be out of town for days and the crocodile would get hungry. The neighbor said he did not feel "safe" and the owner was not being "responsible" and wanted our office to do something about it! So the first part of our title, "Safety Responsibility," may have different meanings to different people.

As Chair of the FRI Committee, I would often preside over meetings or give remarks during various conferences throughout the United States and Canada. At one conference in Ottawa, Ontario shortly after September 11, 2001, I made the following remarks to the group of about 350 people.

· · · · · · ·

On behalf of the FRI Committee, I would like to welcome you to the 2001 Workshop. I hope you en-

joy yourself in Ottawa. We know that things have changed after September 11th. Several active members of the FR Committee had to cancel and not attend the workshop this year.

You know now that the president of the United States and the vice president are no longer allowed to be together in a public place. And they have to fly on separate planes.

I do think that my office went a little too far when my boss, Terry Montalbano, and I had to fly separately to protect the future of FRI in our State. My boss had a nice direct flight from Chicago to Ottawa. I had to take a connecting flight through New York, 800 miles out of the way; maybe they're trying to tell me something.

• • • • • • •

On another occasion, I was giving an opening speech in which we were thanking a member of the AAMVA Staff that was leaving the FRI Committee, Nathan Root. I thanked Nathan and asked him to come up to the stage. I presented him a gift and I asked him to open it in front of all the people. He reluctantly opened the present and revealed a gold clock with an engraving on it. I commented, "Nathan, I learned the hard way not to bring a ticking package on an airplane!" It created quite a laugh.

During these conferences we get well acquainted with DMV employees throughout the country. We often go out during the evening and exchange stories. Here is a sample of some of the things we talk about after hours:

• • • • • • •

- How one state had a program to confiscate vehicles that received multiple tickets for driving without insurance and then "crushed" the vehicle. The lady who told the story said, "I was on vacation and when I heard they were going to crush the first vehicle, my vacation was over. I came right back to work to see it. The TV cameras were there and then came the bulldozer. The vehicle was crushed right in our site. How exciting!"

- Another story was told about an individual who would take out her false teeth and lick them in front of other employees at her desk. The same employee was in a wheel chair and on one snack day, she put a banana under her pants as she wheeled herself back to her desk to eat. The same employee spilled water on her lap and was seen drying herself with a hairdryer. And, you guest it, the hair dryer was placed under her pants. This all occurred at her desk.

- One individual told the story about how their DMV Administrative Office was in the same building as the State Police. We all know State Police Officials are known for their formality and discipline. One day the DMV official received a telephone call from the commissioner who told her he wanted to see her right away on a major issue. He said he would come to her office. A few minutes later, she could hear marching coming from down the hall. She looked out of her office to see three uniformed men coming toward her all in attention and very serious. She thought, "Oh my God, what did we do wrong?" The men entered her office, had a seat, took off their hats, sat in their chairs with their backs straight up, and there was complete silence. Finally, the commissioner spoke. "We have a major violation in code," he said. "Someone in your office posted an unauthorized picture on the wall in the lobby!" Oh, no, anything but that!

· · · · · · ·

That is just a sample of what us DMV employees talk about after hours. Don't you wish you worked for the DMV?

FAST FOOD EMPLOYEES
"THINGS KIDS SAY"

Some things that people say just bug me. You know, they just don't make sense. Sometimes I would like people to just think before they open their mouths. If they did, the world would be a better place.

One thing that bothers me is kids these days are not taught to think. So-called modern technology does all the thinking for them. Sometimes I wonder how smart you have to be to get a job these days. When I was 16 I worked at a fast food hamburger joint in Benton. I had to run the cash register and give change. These days the employee punches in the register how much you gave them, and then the machine tells them how much change to give.

The kids don't learn to think. You give them a five and the meal is $4.50, they have to look at the register to know that the change is 50 cents. That's sad.

Another thing, Have you ever placed an order in a fast food place, and the employee asks you, "Would you like that here or to go today?" They have to add the word "today" to their question. Sure, I want it today. Why in the world would I stand in line and order my food a day in advance. Like, no, I want my food tomorrow at 2 P.M. or next Monday at 3 P.M. Sometimes I wonder where these guys are coming from.

CREDIT CARDS
"EARN THOSE POINTS"

There must be a real big profit these days with credit cards. I receive a new one in the mail every few days. "You have been pre-approved, just sign here, and go out and charge $10,000." And some companies go as far as sending you checks for five or ten grand. All you have to do is to go out and cash them. Spend today, pay tomorrow!

It's very popular for organizations or businesses to sponsor their own credit cards as well. In fact, I charge all my expenses on my airline bankcard. For every dollar I spend, I earn a mile. When I accumulate 25,000 miles, I can cash them in for a free domestic airline ticket.

Some cards offer "cash back" for every dollar charged on their card. Some charities and churches sponsor their own cards to earn donations for every dollar charged. Even universities and local schools are offering their cards as well.

The big push for credit cards got me thinking. With all the aggressiveness these days of funeral home directors, I wouldn't be surprise if they would come out with their own cards. I can see the television commercials now, "Charge It Today, and Don't Pay Tomorrow! Are you fed up with high costs of burying your loved ones? Do you want to go out with a first class funeral, but can't trust your relatives to spend their inheritance on your funeral? Use your charge card and earn one point for every dollar you charge. Your points will add up faster than you can imagine. If you live long enough, you could be charging your way to a free first class funeral. Don't put a burden on your loved ones. After all, you can't trust them anyway. Show them you care. When charging your purchases, use your Smith & Jones Mortuary Charge Card. Charge today, and if you live long enough, you won't have to pay tomorrow!"

Folks, you heard it first here. When you see that commercial for real some day, give me credit, will you? Or, if you are funeral home director, remember my idea is copyrighted! Don't even think about plagiarism!

THE LOST CREDIT CARD
"GOING ONLINE"

Like most people in America, I am addicted to the Internet. I don't know how I survived before I got a computer and learned how to click my way through cyberspace. One day I had a problem with my online Internet provider. I signed onto the system and my account came back invalid. My account was cancelled. I couldn't understand it. After I thought for awhile, I had a good idea what the problem might be.

Here's my story. Two weeks earlier, I lost my credit card. Well, that's not totally true. Really, my wife lost her credit card, and we had the same number. My wife is always losing something. She once reported her credit card lost while we were dating, found it later, and tried to use it to purchase vitamins at a chiropractor's office. The card came back stolen with the message to confiscate the card and call the police. It was a good thing that the lady in the doctor's office was a friend, because if she wasn't my wife-to-be could have ended up in jail!

Nevertheless, we had cancelled our card and our company issued us another one. I had my old number as a direct bill on the computer for my online service. So, in order to avoid a problem, I went online to change my credit card. I did and everything went ok.

I then checked to see when my online service did their monthly billing. I found out that it had occurred three days earlier. I was concerned so I called their customer service number. I explained my situation to them. The clerk indicated that I should be fine and that they would be able to bill me with my new credit card number.

So, you may ask, why was I cancelled? I called the customer service number again after I couldn't sign in. I explained the situation. They indicated that when I called earlier that the billing had gone out and my account cancelled automatically. Cancellations automatically occurred when the bill remained unpaid for three days. However, they had a record that I had telephoned and knew all about my new number. The clerk indicated that they would reinstate me immediately. I asked if they needed my credit card number. They said, "No, we have it in the computer." I again asked, "Why was I cancelled if you have my new number?" He went on to say, "Under those circumstances, you have to call us back, so we can reinstate you manually."

The more I thought about this, the more questions I had. "You mean," I said, "your computers can't override a cancellation with a new credit card number?" And I asked why they did not tell me about that the need for a second phone call, the first time I called?

"You are the largest Internet provider in the United States. You have millions of subscribers. You have millions of dollars in equipment and advanced technology. And you can't type in something to have your computer override a credit card cancellation with a valid one?" I asked.

"You don't understand," the clerk said. "We are in Billing. All the programming is done in our Programming Department."

"Don't any of you folks in billing ever talk to the people in the Programming Department? If you did, you could ask them to correct this problem," I said.

I finally demanded to talk to the supervisor. She went on to repeat everything her employee said. She went on to admit that my problem happened all the time, and they just simply reinstate the customer on the phone after they call back the second time. They do nothing to prevent the account from canceling automatically. And she saw nothing wrong with that.

I just didn't get it. Here we have a billion dollar company and their Billing Department never meets with their Programming Department. They never had the idea to get that changed!

The point of this story, is if your have your credit card cancelled, don't bother to try to prevent your online Internet account from being cancelled. It will. Just wait until after it's done, and then give them your new number. Accounting can't talk to Programming!

SAVE THE ENVIRONMENT
"HELP US SAVE US MONEY!"

Don't you just love it when a business promotes something intended to help you, when they are really helping themselves? For example, some salespeople make you feel that you just can't afford not to buy their expensive item. Not only are you saving a large sum of money, but most of their profit is going to charity anyway (yeah, right!), and our lives would be so much better with the product.

In fact, once I saw an ad for one product when they indicated that a percentage of their profits were going to charity. That part was in big letters. I read the fine print with a magnifying glass, which actually said only 1 percent of their profit was going to the charity. Only 1 percent! What a scandal.

My wife and I stayed at a Chicago hotel for several nights while she was attending a work conference. The price of the room was about twice what we usually pay. For prices like that, we really expect to get something for our money. In the hotel room, there was this nice big blue sign staring at us on the bed as we walked in. It looked like it was saying "Read Me! Read Me!" So, the nice people we are, we picked up the sign and read it. It read as follows:

· · · · · · ·

In our efforts to contribute to our city, country and world environment, we are promoting responsible awareness. (So far this sounds pretty good. They are covering a big area here, city, country and world.)

Since we host guests daily from this country and from around the world, we are using this opportunity to increase their community and environmental involvement through our hotel's Environmental Awareness Program. (This hotel must be really concerned about the environment. They want to show us how **we** can contribute. Wow!)

Our hotel is a community-involved and environmentally aware hotel, participating in community recycling and energy conservation programs. (Not only are they concerned about the environment, they are even concerned about the community. Boy, I'm glad I stayed at this hotel!)

We encourage our guests to join and help save precious natural resources through energy and water conservation.

(Here comes the good stuff!)

Electricity, gas and water are saved by turning off unneeded lights and thoughtful usage of air conditioning and heating. (Now, the focus has left the hotel and is on me. I have to do something to help the environment!)

In our efforts to contribute to the environment through reduced usage of water, electricity and chemicals, your bed linen will be changed every other day during your stay and upon each guest's departure. (So that's the real reason for the letter. They want to get out of changing the sheets. They waited last to sock-it-to-you. And without doubt, their big environmental thing happens to save them money. I wonder how environmentally conscious they would be, if this did not save them money? P.S. I wonder if the maids ever get mixed up on when a guest is departing or staying another night. If they do, then we would be sleeping in the previous guest's sheets.)

If you wish to have your linen changed daily during your stay, please contact Housekeeping. Thank you for your participation. (Who's going to call after all of that, please? I can here someone say. "I'm in Room 202, and I don't want to help the environment, I want my linen changed daily, hell with the planet!")

· · · · · · ·

I would like to know how much money they are saving with this program. And, with the money they saved, did the cost of the rooms go down? How many people lost their jobs because of this policy to save the earth? Did they contribute any of the savings to environmental causes? (I would guess, do you think a whole one percent of the profits?) I don't think so. I'm sure the money went right into the pockets of the hotel owners.

The next time you're in a hotel, call the front desk and request that they change your linen every other day. Help the environment! Save the planet! And, if you can help the hotel make more money, then so be it! Sometimes, what's best for business is also best for us. Everyone wins.

CHAPTER 8

GOOD NIGHT, CHARLOTTE

I got married late in life, at age 35, in December of 1995. My wife is not known for her cooking, her house cleaning, or for following the direction of her husband. Thinking of my married life makes me want to spend some time by myself in that special room.

MY WIFE
"THE DOMESTIC MANAGER"

My wife has a hard time in the kitchen. She tries real hard, but she just can't get it right. She even went to cooking school, and was asked to drop out by the instructor. She was holding everyone else back. When she is trying to cook something, I can hear her a mile away. First, when she gets out the pans, she makes the loudest noises, "Bang, Bing, and Bong!" The pan she's getting is always the one in the back or on the bottom. When she gets started she makes a mess and a half, and then the smoke, and then the smoke detectors go off. Finally, I just throw my hands up and surrender. "It's not worth it, let's go to a restaurant!"

My wife also likes to cut out coupons. She will spend hours going through the newspaper cutting out coupons for various food items. You should see her in the grocery store. She will leave for the store and come back three hours later. She will look up each item we need, compare the prices with or without the coupons. She may spend 15 minutes to decide to buy a small or large portion of one product.

One day she had a $1.00 off coupon for a bag of hotdog buns that we did not need. You know what she did? She saw a lady picking up the product, and sold the coupon to her for 40 cents! Later in line at the cashier, she saw the lady trying to use the coupon, and being turned down because the coupon had a minimum $10 purchase, and all she wanted was a package of hotdog buns. My wife left the store as fast as she could!

Speaking of coupons, I have to tell you the story about the "Welcome Wagon." We both had lived in Springfield about ten years when we moved into a new house. My wife had heard that the Welcome Wagon organization would give people who are new into town a basket full of coupons and gifts. So, you know what she did? She called them and told them that we had moved into a new house. She left out the part that we had been in town for about ten years.

The Welcome Wagon lady met her for lunch. My wife had to sit there and listen to the orientation of Springfield. The lady went over how we have a Convention Center, the State Fair, and directions to the Mall. My wife just sat there and listened, "Now, what street did you say the Mall was on?" she replied. Finally, it got to the good part. The basket full of coupons! There were free car washes, free dinners, etc. Boy, was my wife in hog heaven.

Her justification was that we had not called Welcome Wagon when we first moved here ten years ago, so we had all that free stuff coming. So, folks, if you haven't called Welcome Wagon, give them a call, and tell them Charlotte sent you!

My wife is also known for her "sneakiness." She will always say one thing, but behind my back do another, and hope that I don't find out. I think this started in her childhood when she was raised with two sisters and a brother. I always tell her, "You're not at your parents' house, you're married now!" It doesn't help.

She told me she wanted to lose weight. "I will not eat any desert for the next month." I said, "That's great, honey!" The very next day, I came downstairs quicker than I was expected, to see her eating ice cream out of her glass. She dipped it in her glass so I would not see a bowl in the sink! How clever.

When we were dating, we visited my aunt and uncle in Chicago. I had a key to their home because I stayed there a lot. When we arrived, they had not made it home yet, so we were waiting for them in the living room. Charlotte had not met my aunt and uncle before. While we were waiting, we saw a nice big box of chocolate candies on the table in the living room. I opened the box to see it was full, not one piece missing. I told Charlotte that we should not eat the candy unless we were asked. It was only the polite thing to do. She agreed.

A few minutes later, I went to the rest room. I apparently came out a few minutes too early; Charlotte's mouth was full of chocolate candy. In fact, she almost choked to death. Well, at least she took two pieces, so it would look like we both had a piece.

On another occasion, I came downstairs of our home to see soap suds pouring out of our dishwasher. I asked my wife, "What in the world is going on?" Her response was, as usual, "I don't know." I went on to explain, that for suds to come out of a dishwasher, something had to be put in it. Suds do not come out of a dishwasher for no reason. She finally admitted that she put Soft Scrub in the dishwasher because we were out of dishwashing liquid. We had to stay home and wipe up suds every few minutes because it was pouring out onto the floor. So, the moral of this story: Don't try this at home!

We had the opportunity on one occasion to use our friend's vacation home in Marco Island, Florida. After we had been there a few days, we had gone through several towels. I asked my wife to wash them in the washing machine. The towels were very high quality and they all were white. My wife had a project. A few minutes later, I could hear the washing machine going, so the project was in progress.

About a half-hour later, I heard the buzzer go off on the washing machine. Since I was close by, I opened the machine to place the towels in the dryer. To my amazement, there was only one towel in the washer. One towel? There was a basket full of six or seven additional towels of the same color.

I immediately called Charlotte into the laundry room. "What's going on?" I asked. "Why is there only one towel in the washer?" Her response was, "It said on the label to wash separately!"

Taking Responsibility
"Whose Fault is it?"

My wife will never take responsibility for anything. Whatever happens is never her fault. You won't believe all the excuses she comes up with.

The other day, she was hunting for a certain sweater in her closet. She asked me to help her. We looked and looked, but could not find the sweater. First of all, you should have seen her closet. It was the most unorganized group of things that I have ever seen. Nothing was grouped together. There was no sort of order.

We had lived in our house for about a year at the time. I asked her why her closet was in such a mess. "It's your fault," she said. "When we moved in, I wanted to organize it, but you said we had no time." When we moved in we had hundreds of boxes. I told her to put everything on the rack and come back later to organize it. I wanted to get all the boxes emptied and out of the way. So, a year later, she had never gone back to organize the closet, so now it's my fault!

A few weeks earlier, her sister and family had stayed overnight at our house. On Saturday morning, when I got up, I could hear everyone downstairs. I got out of bed and I smelled a terrible odor. I wondered, "What has she done now?" I got out of bed and went downstairs.

My wife had cooked pancakes for the kids and had set the plastic bowl directly on the burner, while it was still hot. Not only did she burn the plastic bowl, but it was all over our electric stove burner. I asked her how in the world she did that. Her response was that the kids were helping her cook. Her sister quickly spoke up and stated that Charlotte had placed the bowl on the stove, and not her daughters. So, there you have it. My wife was trying to blame that act on the kids. Nevertheless, I had to scrape the burner for about an hour to get all the hard plastic off.

That's not the entire story. You should have seen the pancakes. They were like rubber. They looked like something out of a horror film. I asked her what went wrong. Her response was, "There must have been something wrong with this box of batter!" Of course, my wife must have followed the directions on the box to the letter. It was the batter in the box. I guess we should have written the company.

Speaking of following directions on the box, my wife even messed up a simple dish of macaroni and cheese. I had learned how to fix a box of macaroni and cheese when I was about 12 years old. All you have to do is boil the water, add the stuff, drain it, add butter and milk and you have a nice dish. Every time my wife makes it, she forgets one of the steps.

The other day it was so runny, it was terrible. I asked her what happened. "Nothing," she said. "There must be something wrong with your taste buds," she said. Come to find out, after a brief investigation, my wife couldn't find the drainer in the cabinet, so she tried to drain the water out with the lid. This, of course, left about two extra cups of water. Even after I found her out, she said that her portion of the macaroni and cheese tasted fine. There must be something wrong with me. (Now you may understand while we eat out a lot!)

My wife even blames me, her loving husband, for actions in her dreams. Let me explain. The other night, I woke up to see my wife standing in front of my bed at 2 A.M. with two plates and two forks. I said, "What in the world are you doing?" She had had a dream about food being in our bathroom, and had walked downstairs, in her sleep, and got two plates and two forks. She said that I had asked her in the dream to go downstairs and get the dishes.

I asked her why we would have food in the bathroom, and she had no answer. However, it was my fault, because I had asked her to get the plates. So, when I say something to her in a dream, it's my fault.

Now, do you feel sorry for me as a husband?

I rest my case.

WOMEN'S MAGAZINE
"DANGEROUS WRITINGS!"

Always beware of when your wife mentions that she read something in a "Women's Magazine." My wife is always doing this to me. It's like these magazines are gods. Everything written is true, and is a "must do."

These magazines often provide advice on sex. Once she read that if you have sexual intercourse in a certain position, you can influence the sex of your child. A boy would be one position and a girl in the other. I asked my wife if they guaranteed the results. She replied, "No, the chances are 50/50 for a girl." Oh, how scientific. After you think about it, isn't the chance of getting a boy also 50/50?

My wife read that when you leave for vacation you should place your hot water heater on "Vacation Setting" and you will save all of this money. We were going to St. Paul for a business trip and we were to be gone only a few days. My wife reminded me of the women's magazine. My response was that I did not want to mess with it at this time. We would only be gone for a few days, and we had no time. It was time for us to leave for the airport.

While I was putting the suitcases in the car, I heard the basement door close. I came back and asked my wife what she was doing in the basement. "Nothing," she replied. I said, "Nothing! I saw you come up from the basement. Did you mess with the hot water heater?" "Oh, no," she answered.

I went down into the basement. I smelled gas around the hot water heater. I asked my wife, who always tells the truth, to join me in the basement. I then asked her, "What button did you turn?" She said, "The Vacation Setting button, of course?" I then asked her, "Then, why do I smell gas." "Did you, by chance, touch the on and off button?" Her first response was, "No." However, when she realized that I was getting quite upset, she admitted that she turned it off first, and when she realized that she had made a mistake, quickly tuned it back on.

What she did was turn the gas off, then back on, and then set the Vacation Setting. The hot water heater was waiting for a match to be lit. Gas was escaping. If I had not seen my wife sneak out of the basement, our house could have blown up!

My message to all the husbands out there–look through your home and find every women's magazine you can, and throw them away!

THE CAT AND THE WIFE
"MY TWO GIRLS"

I am a cat lover. Ever since I was a kid, I always re-member having a cat. The cat I had when we first got married was named "Mercedes." I got her about two years before I met my wife.

The way I got this cat was interesting; well, at least I think it is. Two of my friends, Dave and Diane Maulding, were concerned because I lived by my-self. They encouraged me to get a cat. I am known for being conservative with my money, so I did not want to spend any on an animal. I told my friends that if I could find a cat that was fixed, de-clawed, house broken, with all her shots, and FREE, I would take it. A few days later, Dave called me and said, "You won't believe what I read in the paper." There was an ad wanting a good home for a cat, house bro-ken, de-clawed, fixed, with litter box, food, every-thing–all free. The owner was moving out of town and couldn't take the cat with her. So, I had my cat.

My wife is a little jealous of my cat. She often thinks I show the cat more affection and that maybe I love her more. My wife once asked me, "Do you love that cat more than me?" My response was, "I've know the cat longer." Well, I guess that wasn't the right an-swer, or the answer my wife was looking for, because she got a little upset.

When we first got married my cat did not like my wife either. I don't know what it is about women being jealous. One day my cat did jump up in my wife's lap. My wife thought she had finally come around to like her. Charlotte looked at me and grinned. However, a second later, the cat opened her big mouth like a tiger and hissed at her. The cat jumped up in my wife's lap specifically to hiss at her. Well, at least she doesn't hide her feelings.

DATING THE WIFE
"CHANGE OF TASTE!"

Isn't it interesting that when you're not paying for something yourself, your tastes change? When I was dating Charlotte, her taste in food was very interesting. I can explain it in one word, "expensive!" Every time we went out for dinner, she would order the most expensive thing on the menu. She ordered wine with her meal so often, I was getting to wonder if she was an alcoholic. And she would even order deserts. You should have seen the amount on some of the checks!

I just couldn't afford to take her out very much. In fact, I found myself taking her out for dinner less and having her over to my house for dinner more. Most of our dates involved her watching TV at my house, because I was always broke.

She even had the nerve to brag to me about all the money she was saving since she was dating me. She told me that she had purchased several Certificates of Deposit with part of her savings. I understood how she could save so much money, because I was paying for everything! I was broke and she had all of this extra cash.

One day she told me she felt bad about me paying for all the meals, so she invited me over her house for dinner. She's not known for her cooking, so this was rare. After the dinner had cooked for a while, I suddenly saw smoke coming from the oven. "What's that burning?" I asked. She rushed to the oven and the entire meal was ruined. It had burnt to a crisp. (After we married, this scene would repeat itself several more times.)

Since the dinner was history, Charlotte then suggested that we order pizza. We called the order in to a local restaurant. When the pizza was delivered, she acted like she couldn't find her purse to pay for the pizza. I was forced to pay for the dinner! Here I was, invited over to her house because she wanted to pay me back for all the dinners I had purchased for her. How does it end up? I had to pay after all! (You know, she never volunteered to pay me back either.)

Where is it written that the male has to pay for all the dates? I never understood that, or believed in it. I believe it must have started years ago when the women didn't work, but stayed at home waiting for their dates. Can someone tell the ladies today that times have changed? Women today work! And, since women work, why can't they help pay for dates! With equal rights for women and with women making big bucks, it's time for the men in this country to stand up and make a change!

One day at dinner, I asked Charlotte what she usually ordered on the menu when she was by herself. She even had the nerve to admit that she usually ordered the least expensive item on the menu! So, with that, I made up my mind; I had to take a stand. After six months of dating, I told Charlotte that I felt it was time that she start helping pay for some of our dinners. This, may I say, did not go well with my girlfriend. She first went through the "you don't love me stage." I was the evil, unloving boyfriend. However, I was determined to stick to my guns.

I found it interesting that I saw a big change in her eating habits. Now, she had a craving for much cheaper items on the menu. She gave up drinking wine with her meals and had a sudden craving for water with lemon. And, the least expensive item now was much more filling, because she no longer had room for desert.

LEAVING THE WIFE ON A JET PLANE "WELL, JUST IN CASE!"

One thing about my wife, you can never predict what she will say next. In fact, one day I was about to leave on a five-day business trip to Omaha, Nebraska. Charlotte seemed very sad that I was about to leave. However, just before I was about to walk out of the door, she did not say, "Honey, I love you," or "I will miss you," or "Hurry home." Instead, she asked me, "If your plane crashes, do you mind if I marry again in two years?"

CHAPTER 9

OUR DAUGHTER AMANDA

Amanda was born on December 18, 2000. She was quite a blessing for us. We had wanted a child for many years but were unable to deliver. With a baby it is hard to read while in that special room. She is always at the door, knocking or peeping in. However, try your best, so you can finish this book.

THE PREGNANCY
"THE BABY!"

I never thought it was possible to begin raising a family in your forties, however, in this day and age, anything goes. On April 4, 2000, my wife and I heard that we were going to have a baby! It took a while to sink in, because we had almost given up on the idea.

Being new parents-to-be, we signed up for every parenthood class available. In fact, when we finished all the classes, I thought we should qualify for a college degree. During our first class, they explained how the baby was developed, and what to expect during the pregnancy. We got to see and hold plastic babies that represented how big the baby was during different stages of the pregnancy. How neat.

Our second class was full of "don'ts and dos." The instructor told us not to do this and that. She actually scared us both to death. If this baby survives, it will be a miracle. We both took notes and had page after page of things not to do.

I was so confused. I told the instructor that we should just keep the baby home until she was old enough to take care of herself. Everything they mentioned was not safe.

They also showed us slides of the delivery, from which I had to turn my head. And just think, my wife wanted me to be in the room when our baby was born. How would I handle that? I thought I would probably pass out on the floor.

One of the slides was on a baby being circumcised. That was the grossest thing I have ever seen. Again, I had to turn my head. I was glad we were having a girl. When we found out that we were having a girl, I played a joke on my wife. I told her that I wanted to name the baby after my grandmother. I asked her not to fight me on this because I felt strongly about it. Charlotte asked me which grandmother. I told her Gertrude. You should have seen her face. First it turned red, and then there was a long pause. She finally said, "Isn't that name kind of old fashion." Before my wife went into early labor, I told her that I was kidding.

We made it through the classes and we made it through delivery. Amanda was born healthy with no problems. Before we took her home, the nurse told us what to do. Our friend Anne Dossett came over the first day and spent a day with us to help teach us. I never once looked at the notebook full of notes from all of those classes. I think taking care of a baby is something you just do. So, for those future dads, my advice is stay away from the classes! They will just scare you to death!

AMANDA
"THE FIRST YEAR!"

They say if you can make it the first year, all is down hill from there. Well, we made it, but it was not easy. No one told us that a baby cries all the time! We could not believe it. The baby would wake up about every two or three hours, just screaming as if she were dying. The first few nights it would scare us to death.

Charlotte did a good job getting up most of the time. As most men would tell you, getting up in the night is the "woman's job." I had a good excuse because Charlotte was breastfeeding, and I couldn't help Amanda in that area.

This is how the first few days and weeks went: scream, yell, cry, poop, eat, scream, sleep, poop, eat, scream, yell, poop, and eat. This went on and on. I think the neighbors must have thought we were killing the kid. We just could not understand all the crying.

Finally, we got used to it and were able to drown everything out in our minds. When I was single I just hated to go over friends homes that had babies. They were always so loud and the parents just let them scream. I would often think, "Why don't they do something about that screaming!" Now I understand. After a while you just don't hear it any more. It doesn't bother you. The screaming fits in like part of the furniture.

Oh, those diapers. Why is it that baby poop seem to stink a lot worst than adults? I just could not figure this out. You women would be proud of me, because I did do my share of changing Amanda's diapers. I just couldn't understand why she pooped so often. Me, for instance, I go once or twice a day. She would go through about ten diapers a day. Why is that? I think the doctors should invent some type of pill that makes the baby go less often. These diapers are very expensive and are not very pleasant to change.

And, when the baby was sick for the first time, we of course panicked! Call the doctor! Call 911! She has a fever! What do we do? She's going to die! That was the drill. This however only lasted for the first two or three times. After that it too became a routine, at least for me. However, with Charlotte it was always, "She's going to die!" I don't know what it is with mothers, but maybe it is because what they have to go through in delivery. They have more invested than the dad has. The dad just has to sit back and watch. The woman, on the other hand, has to pay back the sin of Eve in the Garden every time a baby is born.

The main thing is we survived the first year, and yes, it was worth it!

AMANDA
"THE TERRIBLE TWOS!"

Our daughter Amanda turned two years old on December 18, 2002. Prior to that time, we did not know what people meant by the two words, "Terrible Twos." We learned the hard way.

During two short years she went from the cutest and most innocent baby in the world to the most demanding and hardheaded baby in the world. She now wanted everything now, and everything had to be her way, or the high way. Even with that, there are still things she says that make us laugh.

The Doll

One day we were going for a walk with the stroller. Amanda had a baby doll with her that would make noises when you moved her. On this day, the doll was making all kinds of noises like a real baby. Amanda looked at us in a frustrating way, and said, "Daddy, will you make this baby doll shut up!"

The House Guests

On another occasion, one of good friends, Gary Strohm, and his family were staying the weekend with us. Amanda was quite excited about having company. We went out to eat and after we had finished, Amanda went to the bathroom and when she returned the three kids were gone (they had gone outside to wait for us). Upon returning, Amanda, with a very serious look, said, "Where did the people go?"

That evening, when we were taking Amanda upstairs to go to bed, on the way up, she said in a crying voice (she didn't want to go to bed), "Good night, people."

The TV Star

One day, we were watching videos of Amanda when she was a baby. She had not seen herself before on television and got very excited. She gave us a big grin and said, "Two Amandas!"

The Birds and the Bees?

Like most kids her age, she had no problem putting her fingers in her mouth. One day while I was driving her home from day care, I told her that she was a big girl and that big girls don't put their fingers in their mouths. She said, "Amanda do it no more." (Of course, a few minutes later, I would see that finger in the mouth again).

Later, she looked at me very seriously and said, "Daddy, can Amanda have a baby?" I thought, oh no, she's not even three yet and she's talking about a baby! I told her, "Oh no, not until you are real big!" Remembering what I had told her a few minutes earlier, she said, "Amanda's big now!"

You have to be careful what you say to a two-year-old; you don't know when it may come back to haunt you!

The Candy Bar Monster

We had been pretty good in keeping candy away from Amanda. We didn't keep candy bars in the house or eat them. In fact, Amanda really didn't know what a "candy bar" was prior to this incident.

At work one day, I was craving chocolate so I bought some small candy bars during lunch and put them in the refrigerator. When I picked up Amanda from day care, I told her that I had a candy bar for her at home. She said, "Amanda don't like candy bars." I thought to myself, "Boy, I am a great parent! I have kept my little girl away from chocolate."

When I got home, I went into the refrigerator and ate another candy bar. When Amanda saw me eating it, she asked for one. After she ate it, she said, "Amanda likes candy bars!"

From that day on, she wanted a candy bar every day when I brought her home from day care. One day I told her, "No, Amanda can't have a candy bar every day." She replied, "But, Daddy, I've been waiting all day!"

Another day, we were in the checkout line at the grocery store. Amanda was in the cart and I was putting all the groceries on the counter top. I looked back a few minutes later and saw Amanda sitting there, eating a big candy bar, with chocolate all over her face. She had reached over the counter, pulled out a candy bar by the register and helped herself big time.

I created a Candy Bar Monster!

AMANDA QUOTES AT AGE THREE
"SAY WHAT?"

These quotes are from the journal we keep on Amanda. They were all taken during her third year on this great planet.

"Mommy, does Jesus help animals grow up?"

"Daddy, I will give you loving later, after we watch TV."

"Mommy, Jesus is going to heal you. Remember how He healed my finger?"

"I will not poo poo on the train. I will not poo poo on Mommy. I will not poop on Daddy. I will not poop on a star. I will not do it anywhere."

"Mommy, you can't sing. Join the circus!"

When asked by Mommy, "What did I do to deserve such a beautiful girl?" Amanda replied, "Got married!"

"Daddy, you're a Chicken Head!"

"My legs, arms, belly button and everything grow really big!"

When we drove by the public utility plant, Amanda asked Daddy, "What is that?" Daddy replied, "It's the power plant." Amanda said, "That's not a plant, it's a house silly."

"Fishes eat fishy food and dolphins eat dolphin food!"

"I like orange juice because it makes me healthy."

"My hair is going to be red, blue and yellow."

When talking to Grandma on the phone, all in one sentence Amanda says, "I miss you so much I'm watching TV, Bye."

Amanda tells Mommy, "You ate your salad. You ate your pizza. That's why you go poop."

"Jesus is everywhere, Mommy says, but Jesus isn't in the bath tub!"

To a perfect stranger in the mall, Amanda said, "My name is Amanda, I have two grandmas!"

After picking Amanda up at day care, out of the blue, she told her daddy, "Boys are supposed to stand up and girls supposed to sit down when they use the bathroom." That was the lesson she learned that day at day care. Well, you have to learn some time.

AMANDA AT AGE FOUR
"BIG GIRL YET?"

Here are additional quotes from the journal we keep on Amanda. It is amazing how much wisdom, humor and common sense she had at age four.

Here are her quotes:

This is one of my favorites, and no, I did not coach her. It occurred during the 2004 Presidential Campaign. I guess she must have heard us talk about how great President Bush was. One day her ball was missing and she was so upset. It was after a big storm in which we had strong winds. I told her that I thought the wind had blown it away. "My ball must have blown to Chicago or somewhere far, far, away," she said. A few minutes later, she added, "If my ball went to the White House, George Bush would give it back because he is a good man. If it went to Kerry's house, he would keep it!"

We try to teach Amanda about the Lord Jesus Christ. Charlotte is very good at reading to her Bible stories before she goes to bed. Amanda often comes up with really good advice. One day she had this little bit of wisdom to say to her mom: "When Daddy said don't go outside, you don't do it. Jesus said don't hit your parents or you will be locked up in jail forever and ever. I'm trying to teach you that Mommy!"

One day around Christmas we saw a deer in the park near our home. Amanda didn't miss anything. She asked with big excited eyes, "Daddy, does Santa live there?"

Another day, out of the blue, she had this to say: "Jesus will give you a prize for being good all day."

Amanda shared this little bit of wisdom with us one day: "God says listen to Mom and do what Dad says. That's the rule." I only wished my wife would believe the last part.

One morning we were having pancakes for breakfast. It was one of Charlotte's good days and the pancakes actually were edible. Amanda said, "Can I mail a pancake to Grandma?"

Looking at a cute guy on TV, Amanda said, "I can't marry him. He lives on TV and I don't know where that is."

It is funny how kids get full and won't finish their meals, but they always have room for other things. One day she said, "My tummy is full, but not too full for desert!"

Charlotte wanted some good night kisses. Amanda told her, "Daddy took all of my kisses. I only have one left to give to you."

The day after we read the Christmas Story to Amanda, she had this to say: "Mommy, Jesus is alive. The angel took the rock away and his mom was so happy."

We moved to a new house in 2004. Out of the blue, Amanda told us, "We live in a white house like George Bush."

We have some raspberry bushes and Amanda just loves to eat the raspberries. She had this to say about it: "Do raspberries grow in summer because they like summer? Does corn grow because it likes summer?"

I asked her to record some sayings for my web site. I gave her the microphone and she came up with this: "Always say please and thank you. Walk and don't run except if you're in the gym or outside."

Trying to convince Amanda to eat her broccoli, Charlotte tried to rely on one of Amanda's favorite's cartoon characters. "Dora eats broccoli," Charlotte said. "Let Dora have my broccoli then," replied Amanda.

My girl is so modest. "I can't help but be cute. Jesus made my hair and body this way."

When Amanda wouldn't wear a t-shirt her mother bought her, Charlotte said, "My heart is broken!" Amanda was too smart to buy that. She replied, "If your heart were really broken, you would be sick and throw up!"

When our cat Mercedes died, Amanda said, "Mercedes is in Kitty Heaven and Grandpa is in Grandpa Heaven."

When we went to the Lincoln Presidential Museum grand opening in Springfield Illinois, we saw a Lincoln impersonator. Amanda went up to him an asked him, "What is your name?" He replied, "I'm Abraham Lincoln." Amanda then replied in a non-believing tone, "My daddy told me Abraham Lincoln was dead!"

This is one of my favorites. "How did God paint the sky?" Amanda asked. "Did He have a ladder?"

"Mommy, I could make the house look really pretty if I had a magic wand."

"Mommy, how many kitties do cats have when they get married?"

"Did Jesus get wine from there?" Amanda asked as we drove passed a liquor store. Charlotte had read her the story a few days earlier on how Jesus turned water into wine.

One day I got Amanda a kite and she had a good time trying to fly it. Later she had this to say: "A kite will take you up to the moon, but you will have to have a long string."

One day I was upset and raised my voice at Charlotte. Amanda told me this: "Don't yell as Jesus. If you do, you're to tell Jesus that you're sorry for your sins."

Amanda was sitting in my lap. She asked me how old she would be on her birthday. I said five. She then asked how old the following year. I said 6. I told her that it was like counting it would increase by one each birthday. She then asked, "When I'm six will I be big?" I said, "Yes, you will be a big girl." She then replied, "Will I be big enough to get my driver's license?"

When Mommy was upset over something that happened at work, Amanda said, "Mommy, don't think about work. Think about rainbows and Jesus and other good things." What good advice.

"Mommy, when can I have a brother?" Charlotte said, "I'm too old to have another baby!" Amanda then asked, "Can I have a baby?" "When you are older and get married," Charlotte replied. Amanda then said, "Can I marry Daddy? He is so sweet and precious. He makes my heart true." (No I did not coach her to say that!)

In 2005 we decided to host a foreign exchange student. When we explained this to Amanda, she said, "I've been praying to Jesus for a brother and He answered me."

CHAPTER 10

OUR SON HORST

In July of 2005 Charlotte and I decided to have a son. We didn't want to go through the pregnancy or the whole baby thing. In fact, we decided to have a teenager. We hosted an exchange student from Germany through the ASSE International Student Exchange Program.

PICKING HORST

In the summer of 2005 we were at home in Benton, Illinois for the July 4th holiday. I noticed a newspaper ad in the *Benton Evening News* asking for host families for the ASSE International Student Exchange Program. There web site was ASSE.com, easy to remember because of the first three letters. I put the site to memory and ran it up on the computer when I returned to Springfield, Illinois.

I sent an e-mail of interest and was contacted the next day. All I did was ask for more information and these people wanted to sign me up right away. They were really eager beavers. First they called me, then flooded me with e-mails and then they visited my home.

Picking an exchange student was like shopping on line. We actually felt kind of guilty. We went through a list of photos of kids with personal profiles of their interests, their grades, etc.

Actually only one student stood out to us. He was from Germany. He was 16 and would be a junior in high school. He had blond hair, blue eyes, was crazy about computers, designed his school web site, was interested in theater, had a 5 year old sister, and liked to cook, mow the grass and clean house. Since we needed a babysitter, someone to mow the grass and cook, the decision was made. Horst, we want you, we need you!

Is he too good to be true? Well, time will tell. Read on.

THE ARRIVAL
THE BAGGAGE CLAIM EXPERIENCE

On August 23, 2005 we welcomed Horst Wenzel from Dortmund, Germany to the Wayman Family! Horst is an exchange student. He will be with us for the entire school year. He will be a junior at Rochester High School.

Horst does speak good English; however, he is getting a few words mixed up. One word, in particular, created quite a stir at the Abraham Lincoln Airport in Springfield. When we were waiting for the luggage to come off of the plane, in the luggage claim area, we were exchanging small talk Horst was asking us about our house and our family. One question he asked really got our attention. "Do you have a gun?" Horst asked. Charlotte and I looked at each other with shock and amazement. You don't mention the word "gun" at the airport, we thought. Quietly we said, "No, we don't have any guns."

However, he saw the expression on our faces and, thinking we did not understand, he said real loud, "Do you have a GUN?" I told him to keep his voice down as several people turned their heads looking at us. I then quietly asked Horst, "What is your definition of a gun?" He replied, "You know, a place where you plant flowers." I said, "Oh, you mean 'garden'?" "Yes", he replied. He had gotten the two words mixed up. We were lucky that security did not hear us. If so, we would have spent some time with the police.

TRIP TO WAL-MART
CAN I BORROW YOUR RUBBER?

The second day was busy because first we had to go to school to register. I took him to the Rochester High School. First we met the principal and then the administrative staff. Everyone was quite excited to meet Horst and to have another exchange student from Germany. Horst is good looking and the girls all turned their heads when he walked down the hall. And when he spoke, the accent nearly charmed their socks off.

That afternoon we went to lunch and I talked to Horst about the various rules we have in the Wayman household. I spoke about asking permission to have kids over, no phone calls after 10 P.M., that we must know where he is at all times–no sex, drugs, or rock n' roll! I went over the typical things one would for a 16-year-old teenage boy.

After that, Horst and I went to Wal-Mart to get supplies for his school. He picked out some paper, some notebooks, some pens and pencils. He then asked me, "Where are the rubbers?" I looked at him quite shocked, especially since we had just had the talk about the "birds and the bees."

He looked at me and seemed surprised of my look on my face. Again, in a louder voice, he said, "Rubbers!" "What do you mean, Horst? Didn't you listen to anything we talked about during lunch?" I said.

Horst seemed shocked of my reaction. I then asked him to clarify his meaning of "rubber." He then said, "You know, what you use to rub out the pencil marks." "Oh," I said with relief, "you mean 'erasers'!"

I told him that whatever you do, don't ask the teacher, "Can I borrow your rubber. I left mine at home!"

AMERICANS FROM MARS, GERMANS FROM VENUS

After only a few days with Horst it became evident that there is a big cultural difference between Germany and the United States. I often wondered if we were from the same planet.

It seems like the teenagers in Germany have more responsibility and more freedom than the teenagers in the United States. The first big distinction is the drinking age. In Germany, the drinking age is 16 years old. Is alcohol a problem in Germany? According to Horst, drinking is no big deal because it is legal.

At school in Germany, the students take part in the decision-making process for school rules and guidelines. In the United States, it seems like our rules are controlled by the latest school shooting or threat of a law suit.

Horst illustrated this point by telling me his version of the "Macaroni and Cheese" story. During lunch in the Commons area at Rochester High School, *one very small* piece of macaroni and cheese was spotted on the floor. In Germany, it would have simply been picked up and thrown away. However, in the United States it is a major production. It is an accident waiting to happen. It is a potential law suit, a violation of the clean floor policy and the clean air act all rolled up on one. It was a critical moment in time. Horst felt that perhaps he should yell: "Run for your life! We all are going to die!"

However, the Principal handled it very professionally and by the book. First he yelled, "STOP!" He immediately secured the crime scene by placing his entire body as an X around the macaroni and cheese. He was willing to sacrifice his body for the safety of his students. How heroic! He ordered the students to stay away from the crime scene, while at the same time talking on his communications device to the janitor, "We have macaroni and cheese in the Commons area! Clean it up IMMEDIATELY!" The Principal unselfishly stayed at his post, directing the students around the crime scene until the janitor took over and cleaned up the *one* piece of macaroni and cheese. After the clean-up, the janitor placed two large signs in the area, "WET FLOOR," to avoid any injuries or law suits. In less than a half hour the incident was over. The crime scene was cleaned up. No one died. No one was injured. There were no law suits.

Turning the page to another cultural difference, in Germany there are little if no restrictions on the language used by students. It is not necessarily considered bad for students to use the "F" word at school or to see nudity on television. While attending a school open house, Horst's Drama teacher Mr. Shaw told the parents this story. During class Horst was acting out an impromptu scene of someone getting angry. He was really getting into the part and doing an outstanding job. Then suddenly during the speech he used the "F" word! Then at the very same moment, all thirty students in the class room turned their heads to look at Mr. Shaw, who was sitting in the back of the classroom. The students all had their mouths opened sending the non-verbal message, "He used the F word!" Horst could not figure out what was wrong. After class Mr. Shaw had to explain to him that in the United States you don't use the "F" word in school. After all this is Rochester, Illinois, not the Bronx!

The students in Germany get to school differently than in the United States. They take the mass transportation system either by bus or train to their school. There are no "yellow school buses" like in the United States. Again, the kids are treated more like adults. During Horst's first day at school he was faced with a dilemma. Would he accept a ride by car home from school by a beautiful girl, or would he take the yellow school bus. He took the yellow school bus because he was so excited about riding it. Horst said, "Just like in the American movies!"

Horst likes to cook and we allow him to cook many of our meals. As you know by reading my chapter on Charlotte, my wife isn't known for her cooking. One day he asked us, "Do you have any mice?" Well, I certainly hope not, was my immediate thought. But, knowing Horst, I was sure he had another of his words mixed up. He tried to explain it to me, but after looking through our pantry, he found it. Do you know what it was? It was a can of corn. The Indians called corn maize. He thought that "mice" was the root word for it.

On another day, Horst was in the kitchen and he saw me using the electric can opener. "Oh, that is what that is?" He had been opening cans using our old-fashion manual opener. Electric can openers in Germany must not look like the ones in the United States.

Horst also loves our refrigerator because it has an automated ice machine on the outside with the choices of two types of ice. In Germany they do not have that. They have to get their ice by opening the door.

So if you are a teenager reading this and envious of the kids in Germany because of the drinking age and nudity, remember that they do not have ice machines on their refrigerators!

THE MANY FACES OF HORST

When we first picked Horst from the ASSE Exchange Catalog of Kids, we actually felt sorry for him. The mug shot photo showed a kid with very white skin and blond hair. We called it the "Albino photograph." In fact when the coordinator from ASSE discussed him with us she mentioned that several of the families didn't want Horst because of his looks. We actually felt sorry for the poor lad.

When we had decided on Horst we called the ASSE Coordinator. We were concerned that perhaps another parent had entered the "competition" and had selected Horst. We wanted to be first in line. "No, don't worry about that," she said. We were the only family interested in "poor white Horst."

After we picked Horst, we receive an additional packet of photos. Each photo he looked different. He went from the albino kid to the handsome model. What is going on? I have never seen someone that looked so different. Later, Horst explained that in the photo he was going to use he had a bathing suit on. When you cropped it to a mug shot it looked like he was naked. The ASSE Coordinator in Germany made him go to a photo booth to get another photo. This resulted in the Albino photo.

We later found out that Horst is madly in love with a young lady named Anna Sadowski. ASSE also told him not to mention any of that in his profile or literature submitted to the United States. "They will not want someone with a girl friend!" Boy, the ASSE in Germany really was on top of everything, weren't they?

When Horst arrived in the United States we learned that he was not only a good-looking kid but a very charming one as well. The school nurse told me that he was a "Chick Magnet." Not only is he "cute," his German accent drives the girls crazy. If I only knew that when I was in high school I would have talked with a German accent!

One day at school a girl spoke German to Horst. She did such a good job, Horst told her she deserved a hug. After he gave her a hug, several girls started lining up for hugs as well. Even one or two guys were in line. Finally, the school authorities had to get involved to break up the scene. I am sure there is some rule or law against this. Maybe someone would sue if he hugged too hard and broke a rib or two.

STUPID QUESTIONS ASKED TO HORST

Horst received a number of notable questions during his visit to the United States. Most of these came from students at Rochester High. Here are a few to amaze you.

Do they have shoes in Germany?

A girl was complementing Horst on his shoes and asked him if he got those shoes in the United States. Horst said yes, she then asked, "Do they have shoes in Germany?" Horst, then replied, "No, we don't have shoes or streets. We walk on grass all the time so we don't need shoes." The funny part is that the girl actually believed him. Can you imagine her going home to her parents that night, "Mom, Guess what? They don't wear shoes in Germany."

Do they mostly speak English in Germany?

A lady was talking to Horst about all of the different dialects they have in Germany. She indicated that she heard that each province have their own unique dialect. "Yes," replied Horst. He was then asked, "Don't they mainly speak English though?" "Yes," said Horst, jokingly, "English and Chinese are the two biggest languages. They only speak German in their sleep."

Do they have water in Germany?

This question came when a student saw Horst drinking a bottle of water. "Do they have water in Germany?" the student asked. "No," replied Horst, "we shower with ketchup."

Isn't it hard to live under a regime of Adolf Hitler?

This question was asked by one student. I guess he missed the history lesson in which they mentioned the year that Adolf actually ruled Germany.

Isn't Europe an independent Country?

Many Americans seem to be unaware that Europe is a continent! Europe is not a country!

I thought they used the Euro in Europe not Germany?

When Horst bought a shirt at a local department store in Springfield the cashier saw some Euros in his wallet. After Horst mentioned that he was from Germany, the clerk was confused. "I thought Euros were used in Europe, not Germany!" Maybe Germany is a continent, too?!

MORE ON HORST

This chapter on Horst was written after he had only been with us for three weeks. He will actually be here for 40 more weeks! He is with us for the entire school year, ten months! I think it is safe to say that we will have a lot more material on Horst by the end of the school year. It will be quite an experience for all of us.

Look for more on Horst in my next book!

However, for the record Horst is a very special young man. The Wayman family loves him very much, just like our own son. We look forward to a life time relationship with him.

APPENDIX

SOMETHING TO *THINK* ABOUT!

I often think about a scene from one of my favorite movies with actor Jimmy Stewart in which he says, "You know how great it is to finally see daylight after going through a long dark tunnel? Try to live your life as if you were coming out of a dark tunnel." I always thought that was a refreshing way to look on life. A way to appreciate everything we have and everything we see.

Along the same lines, another one of my favorite quotes goes like this: "When you're in a dark room, you bring in light. The entrance of light forces the exit of darkness." There is something magical about light.

And in the Bible, in the book of Matthew, it says, "Neither do men light a candle, and put it under a bushel, but on a candlestick; and it giveth light unto all that are in the house. Let your light so shine before men, that they may see your good works, and glorify your Father which is in heaven." We live in a world full of darkness. God intended for His Children to be the light of the world. God intended our light to shine before man. When we do, it glorifies our Father in Heaven.

For our light to shine, we must first put our faith and trust in the Lord Jesus Christ. We all know John 3:16, "For God so loved the world, that he gave his only begotten Son, that whosoever believeth in him should not perish, but have everlasting life."

Believe in Him. Put your faith in him then let your light shine!

Epilogue

I hope you enjoyed my book. Now that you have completed it, congratulations! Just think how many times you must have done your business while you read my book. The pages may be a little worn and may have the wrong type of smell to it. So, I suggest that you get another copy for your library.

Copies are available through my web site, *http:// www.gordonwayman.com*. Visit me online today. Send me an email with your comments. I look forward to hearing from you.

As an experienced public speaker, I plan to bring my live version of *"While You Do Your Business"* to audiences everywhere through motivational and humorist presentations. If you would like me to speak to your group or organization, contact me for additional information at: gordon@gordonwayman.com.

Thanks again for reading my book. Spread the word.

INDEX

BIOGRAPHY

Gordon Wayman was born on March 30, 1960 in Benton, Illinois. Gordon was the second son for his parents Jack and Helen Wayman. He has one brother, Garry Wayman, who lives in Benton today. Gordon married Charlotte Thomas of Belleville, Illinois in 1990. His father died in 2000, four months before Gordon's daughter Amanda was born. Gordon, Charlotte and Amanda live in Springfield, Illinois.

Growing up in Benton, Illinois, Gordon learned traditional family, small town values. His family took him to church every Sunday morning and Wednesday evening. His father was the owner and operator of "The Dairy Cup," an ice cream stand in Christopher, Illinois (seven miles from Benton.) Every weekend, as a child, Gordon and his brother Garry would go with their mother in the evening to help out at the ice cream stand. Gordon waited on his first customer when he was about 10 years old.

His father went into the Real Estate Business when Gordon was 15. Jack was instrumental in getting Hardees to locate in Southern Illinois and sold locations for them in seven different towns back in 1975.

Gordon delivered newspapers during his teen years in Benton. He actually had three paper routes for the "Benton Evening News." Later on he worked at Hardees and became a "Shift Leader." He received the "Employee of the Month" award two months in a row.

In Junior High School, Gordon served on the Student Counsel. In High School he was active in student government, mainly as a rebel writing letters to the editor against the "oppression" of the school administration and how the school treated the students like "prisoners" with "no freedom." Gordon ran for Student Counsel President his senior year.

Gordon became active in politics with the Republican Party during the 1976 campaign of local candidate for Sheriff, Ron Summers. In 1978, he was the County Coordinator for George Albert Williams' campaign for State Senate. He started the Franklin County Teenage Republican Club and later the county Young Republicans. Also in 1978, Gordon received a statewide award as the "Outstanding Teenage Republican for Illinois." At age 18 Gordon was elected Precinct Committeeman for Precinct 7 in Benton. He served six years in that position.

In 1978 he graduated from High School and attended Southern Illinois University in Carbondale, Illinois. While there he was President of the SIU College Republicans. He started a newsletter "The Southern Illinois GOP Reporter" that went out to over 20 county precinct committeemen and party activists. In 1979 Gordon received the WMCL Radio "Community Service Award." In 1980 Gordon was appointed Illinois Page for the GOP National Convention in which Ronald Reagan was nominated for President. In 1984 Gordon received 21,212 votes and was elected Alternate Delegate to the Republican National Nominating Convention.

Gordon worked professionally for several candidates as Campaign Manager and as a paid consultant. He managed Pete Prineas' campaign for U.S. Congress in 1982 and Miki Cooper's campaign for State Representative in 1984. He served as a political consultant for Vic Koenig in 1984 during an exploratory process to run for U.S. Congress. He was county coordinator for Jim Thompson for Governor and worked in all the campaigns of Jim Edgar for Secretary of State and Governor.

Gordon graduated from SIU in 1982 with a degree in Political Science and Communications. He went to Graduate School for his Masters in Political Science for one year. He attended the University of Illinois at Springfield taking courses towards a Master's Degree in Communications from 1985 to 1987.

In 1984 Gordon started his career in the Office of the Illinois Secretary of State. He served as Court Liaison for the Driver Services Department for the Southern Illinois District from 1986–88 and traveled throughout the state. He became Assistant Manger for the Safety and Financial Responsibility Section (S & FR) for Driver Services in 1988. He has served as Manager of S & FR since 1990. Gordon was elected International Chair for the Financial Responsibility Insurance Committee for the American Association of Motor Vehicle Administrators in 1988 and served for four years.

Gordon and his family are active in church and attend Grace Bible Chapel in Springfield, Illinois. He is the past editor of their newsletter and designed their web site. Gordon is currently a volunteer for the new Abraham Lincoln Presidential Library and Museum in Springfield, Illinois.

In July 2005 Gordon started *Wayman Communications* where he creates and writes web site pages for businesses.

His business web site is
www.waymancommunications.com

He has an extensive personal web site at
www.gordonwayman.com

Contact Gordon Wayman at
www.gordonwayman.com
or order more copies of this book at:

TATE PUBLISHING, LLC

127 East Trade Center Terrace
Mustang, Oklahoma 73064

(888) 361 - 9473